The VEGETARIAN CHEF

The
VEGETARIAN
CHEF

Mastering the Art of
RECIPE-FREE COOKING

Susan Crowther

Foreword by Master Chef Roland G. Henin

PHOTOGRAPHY

by Julie Fallone

PAINTINGS AND DRAWINGS

by Maisie Crowther and the Brattleboro Senior Center

Water-based Media Group, and Marcia Fagelson

Skyhorse Publishing

Copyright © 2015 by Susan Crowther

All Rights Reserved. No part of this book may be reproduced in any manner without the express written consent of the publisher, except in the case of brief excerpts in critical reviews or articles. All inquiries should be addressed to Skyhorse Publishing, 307 West 36th Street, 11th Floor, New York, NY 10018.

Skyhorse Publishing books may be purchased in bulk at special discounts for sales promotion, corporate gifts, fund-raising, or educational purposes. Special editions can also be created to specifications. For details, contact the Special Sales Department, Skyhorse Publishing, 307 West 36th Street, 11th Floor, New York, NY 10018 or info@skyhorsepublishing.com.

Skyhorse® and Skyhorse Publishing® are registered trademarks of Skyhorse Publishing, Inc.®, a Delaware corporation.

Visit our website at www.skyhorsepublishing.com.

10 9 8 7 6 5 4 3 2 1

Library of Congress Cataloging-in-Publication Data is available on file.
ISBN: 978-1-63220-329-8
e-ISBN: 978-1-63220-755-5

Cover design by Abigail Gehring

Printed in China

Appreciation and gratitude extend to the following people

Technical Gratitude~

The Brattleboro Senior Center Water-based Media Group, led by Maisie Crowther, and my mommy, Marcia Fagelson: for their prolific and enthusiastic contribution of the illustrations; Julie Fallone, food photography: for her intuitive culinary images and chronic Getting of me; Coni Porter, initial book design and layout: for teaching me how to sail the ship (and often supplying the wind); Tanya Taylor Rubenstein, loving drill sergeant: for pushing me to Get Serious while honoring my voice; Bernice Mennis, editor, teacher, and gentle mentor: for walking into the Brattleboro Food Co-op on the day that I really *really firmly* decided that I was either quitting this project *for good* or else God had better do *something*; Jim Fallone, publishing guru: for guiding me through the self-publishing (and then publishing) process and offering experience and wisdom that would have taken me years to compile; Carolyn Kasper, neighbor and art-pal: for answering every single solitary design question with patience, kindness, and ease. Happy thanks extend to Abigail Gehring Lawrence for . . . well, *liking my book!~* and giving it a chance. Ms. Gehring and Skyhorse Publishing have been supportive, courteous, and generous with integrity, every step of the way. Hokey be damned: thank you, for making my dream come true.

> *I'm published! I'm a real author!!*

Inspirational Gratitude~

Marlene Beadle, of Marlene's Market and Deli: providing the environment and experience for the original concept; Desha Peacock, creator of *The Desha Show*: for following her dream and reminding me to move along my path; Jim & Julie (again) Fallone: for their encouragement, advice, humor, bizarre forms of empathy, and endless band names; Tiffany Williams, who always spent some of her own tutorial time asking me about my project and encouraging me. Thanks, gal. Michelle Liechti: for believing in me and recommending me to her good friend, Abigail; Julie Forsythe: in breath and smile; Robert Sargent Fay, mentor and friend: for being a staunch defender of integrity; Kathy D'Alessio, life coach, big sister, and Italian ballbuster: for providing the external belief when I kept *86*ing mine away; Lucas my son: for remembering that I was writing a book and actually asking me once or twice about how the project was going (a typically cognitively impossible feat for an 18-year-old American male); and to huzzy Mark Crowther, proofreader, egger-onner, and *etc. police*—identifying 47 unnecessary etceteras. Also, for keeping the coffee hot and in the mug while I sat on my duff and finished the albatross.

For Sam,

who started it all.

Keep pushing, son.

Special gratitude extends to~

the excellent chefs, formerly of the
Culinary Institute of America (CIA), Century Plaza, and Café du Parc:
Master Chef Roland Henin, Chef Bagna,
Master Chef Raymond Hofmeister, and Chef Pierre Latuberne.

Your excellence makes the culinary

world a finer kitchen.

Thank you.

Table of Contents
THE VEGETARIAN CHEF

FOREWORD BY MASTER CHEF

    ROLAND G. HENIN. ix

INTRODUCTION 1

    Why Recipe-Free Cooking? 5

    Let's Get Cooking 8

THE BASIC PHILOSOPHIES 11

    Mise En Place 13

    Seven Virtues of Cooking 17

    Top Ten Tips in the Kitchen 34

THE BASIC INGREDIENTS 45

    What's in a Recipe? 47

    Top Ten Lists. 50

    To Meat or Not to Meat? 56

    Top Ten Ingredients 59

    Seasoned with Accomplishment 80

THE BASIC PROCEDURES 81

    Three Basic Steps. 83

    Salads: The Tip of the Iceberg 90

The Vegetable Rainbow. 95

Amazing Grains and Simple Sugars 103

Cooking Grains 109

The Magical Fruit 115

Stone Soup 118

Making Soup from Scratch 121

Dancing, Swinging, Poetry . . . Marinade . . . 133

Sauces and Spreads and Dips: Oh My!. 141

THE BASIC BEVERAGES. 143

    The Good, the Bad, and the Smoothie. 145

    Coffee, Tea, or Me?. 149

    The Non-Milk of Human Kindness 158

BEYOND THE BASICS. 159

    Mish Mash. 161

    Wild Things. 174

    Rosemary 180

HOW TO FOLLOW A RECIPE. 185

INDEX. 189

FOREWORD BY MASTER CHEF ROLAND G. HENIN

Well . . . with all of this hysteria related to foods in America—some good and some bad—it was bound to finally happen. Someone *in this country* just wrote a fabulous book about foods and what is the most important part of the cooking process. Recipe-free cooking . . . What a "novel" idea! And from Susie Crowther, a former student, on top of that . . . simply amazing!

Yes, I say "finally," because the last one in existence—as far as I know, possibly the *only one* that has ever existed—was written in the 1960s by an extraordinary chef: *Ma Gastronomie*, by Fernand Point, Chef Owner of La Pyramide in Vienne, in the suburb of Lyon. La Pyramide was, in Chef Point's day, possibly one of the very best restaurants in the world and where many of the "Bocuse Gang" famous chefs did their apprenticeships.

❧   ❧   ❧

It is simply amazing that, today, so many people cook strictly by recipes, as this is so unnatural—so mechanical, so anticlimactic. Hell, even a computer, I am sure, could be programmed to do it. And, the big question is, really, *why is this?*

I would certainly understand an apprentice starting out in the profession—a beginner cook, someone just starting out in the kitchen—using recipes as a guide, as a crutch possibly, such as the two training wheels that came with my young son's first bike. But guess what? As soon as he got his balance figured out, as soon as he felt that he could express his own decisions, his own will, and own control over his bike . . . then *off* the training wheels went.

Sure, he fell down a few times and came home with some bruised knees. But eh, there is no free lunch, and this was a small price to pay for his learning and independence. You should have seen him a year or so after that switch, managing to drive his bike simply from torqueing his torso and legs—not even using the handle bars.

What I am saying is very simple.

Cooking with recipes, when you have passed a certain point, such as getting a good handle on the basics, is really like "Painting by the Numbers," as you are simply "assembling some foods together" without any input from *you* into the process . . .with absolutely *no feelings* whatsoever. You are basically an *automate*, not thinking much about what you are doing, not having any contribution in the process or on the outcome, not imparting much of anything personal.

Let's face it. You are simply assembling ingredients like way too many people are doing every day of their lives, producing a dull, boring, uninspired meal. You should consider that cooking . . . yes, cooking . . . should create pleasure and is truly and purely an *act of love.*

Cooking is an act of love—in which you really do not measure or calculate anything—not the time that it takes, not the efforts, certainly not the return on the investment or whatever. You're doing what your feelings are telling you to do, and what it takes to do it right—to create that pleasure in others, to make people happy.

This is what cooking is all about.

&a.   &a.   &a.

Sure, there is going to be a short "interim period," when you are still in need of the recipe, most likely as a refresher, or when you are afraid that something might just not turn out as you would expect. **But trust me on this:** *The sooner you allow your feelings to guide you after you've understood the basic principles of cooking, the sooner you'll become more confident and creative.*

It will not happen overnight, guaranteed. Does any of the good "stuff"? But soon enough, your confidence will grow, without the use of the "recipes crutch," and you will definitely feel on top of the world.

This book may not be for everybody. There will always be people who are "addicted" to recipes. But *you* are *special* and you can do it. Give it a shot and enjoy the company, which is really the whole idea of sharing a meal.

In good cooking . . . Always. —R.G.H

Roland G. Henin, one of approximately sixty Certified Master Chefs in the United States, serves as corporate chef for Delaware North Companies. His responsibilities include serving as a mentor to the culinary teams of all Delaware North properties, challenging their skills and encouraging them to strive for excellence. In addition, virtually all of the company's high-profile events—ranging from The Ahwahnee's Bracebridge Christmas pageant to the 2004 Democratic National Convention to the 2010 opening of New Meadowlands Stadium—have his mark on them.

Prior to joining Delaware North in 1998, Chef Henin was the director of the Culinary Arts Department at the Art Institute of Seattle. Before that, he held various teaching positions at the Culinary Institute of America in Hyde Park, N.Y., and Johnson & Wales College in Providence, R.I.

In 1992, he served as the coach of the gold medal U.S. Culinary Team, helping the American chefs bring home the World Cup from Luxembourg. A teacher and mentor to such famous chefs as Thomas Keller, Chef Henin received in 1993 the first National Chef Professionalism Award ever granted by the American Culinary Federation. Delaware North made its first Culinary Olympic appearance in 2008 under his guidance. Also in 2008, he was named the coach of the U.S. team slated to compete in January 2009 in the Bocuse d'Or in Lyon, France.

Chef Henin was educated at the College Moderne in Nancy, France. He was designated a certified executive chef in 1979 and a certified culinary educator in 1982 by the American Culinary Federation. In 1983—the same year Ms. Crowther began her studies at the Culinary Institute of America—Chef Henin earned the coveted honor of Certified Master Chef.

INTRODUCTION

The Vegetarian Chef arrived some 20 years ago, when Sammy was born. I won't speak for all mommies, but for me, childbirth has been the catalyst for some pretty major life-changing stuff (excluding the arrival of a baby, which should be quite enough). I moved and started a catering business when my second boy was born. And when my first son arrived, I wrote this book.

Inspiration arrived abruptly one day (more abruptly than my son, whom I pushed for four hours—sigh). I was working at Marlene's Market and Deli, a Natural Foods store near Seattle. An excited customer approached me for help. She planned to make Cream of Cauliflower soup. With recipe in hand, she pointed to an unusual ingredient: Mellow White Miso. Did we carry it? We didn't carry that particular flavor, although we did carry about 30 other varieties. As I showed her all the options, I could sense her growing frustration. She continued shaking her head as we walked down the aisles. Without the Mellow White Miso, there would be no Cream of Cauliflower soup. And just like that, she jettisoned her plans of cooking and left discouraged.

Despite being able to choose over 30 available misos, she could not be convinced to substitute. It was a depressing and revolutionary moment. I realized how stifled some people feel about cooking. They are confined—slaves to recipes. Their only way into cooking is through someone else's words, processes, and combinations—in short, someone else's authority. My anger with, not her, but a culture that raised a mindset like hers, ignited. An internal ranting began:

What the hell has happened to cooking? Where has it gone? Nobody cooks anymore! All they do is order take-out and buy pre-made stuff! They've traded in their kitchens for microwaves, restaurants, and reality culinary shows. Our crazybusy culture leaves cooking in the dust. Nowadays, people only cook for special occasions—and then, it's more pain than pleasure having to make 10 trips to 5 stores to buy all the select ingredients to create some controlled combinations of traditional recipes using stuff that's grown thousands of miles away. . . .

Pretty pissed, I admit. But I wasn't doing much about it other than ranting. And besides, it was pretty easy for me to growl and judge, having been to culinary school and logging about two decades of cooking under my belt. Easy to preach when I knew how to cook and felt as comfortable in the kitchen as most people do with . . . well . . . anything that they've spent over 10,000 hours doing!

Preaching aside, our modern culture *has* changed its relationship to cooking. Cooking is not simply a lost art or hobby; it goes much deeper than that. Cooking is a lost survival skill. I felt it was important to create a book that taught one how to cook versus how to follow a recipe.

About nine months later, *The Vegetarian Chef* was born. I submitted it to a few agents and publishers, gathered my rejections, and even received few replies that showed interest. Thinking I could do better, I waited for the tastier offer. That waiting turned into 20 years. Publishing a book sat on the back burner while the crazybusy culture took hold: parenting, full-time working, moving and buying houses, while navigating through a bevy of husbands and boyfriends.

> *Cooking is not simply a lost art or hobby; it goes much deeper than that. Cooking is a lost survival skill.*

Fast forward to recently. My mother-in-law Maisie was diagnosed with cancer. During her treatments, she stopped working. The extra time offered opportunities for reflection. I remember one day distinctly. We were sitting at her kitchen table. On the table and chairs, stacked on the floors, and spread out on counters lay several projects. Maisie described the amount of work it would take to complete each one. At one point in the conversation, she stopped. She took a deep breath and let it release.

"My whole life feels like *unfinished business*." She sighed deeply from what seemed to be the bowels of her spirit. Her arms dropped to her sides, and she took another deep breath. She stared directly at me—an unusual behavior for this Mayflower matron.

It was right around this time that I was reading *Anatomy of the Spirit,* by Carolyn Myss. Myss, a medical intuitive, discusses the correlation of diseases to particular spiritual quests or tasks. The task around the disease of cancer seems to be about unfinished business and the regret that lingers around this. When Maisie blurted this out (unprompted and with no previous reference to C. Myss), an ominous tone resonated.

I heard her.

I decided then and there to publish this book. I consider it one of my babies. I gave it life and then kept it safely hidden. I'm grateful to have mustered the courage to see it launch. *Baby* is 22 years-old; it's time to leave the nest!

The ultimate goal of *The Vegetarian Chef* is to teach people how to cook versus how to follow a recipe. It's a common sense and creative approach to cooking that focuses on pragmatics, intuition, and integrity. It describes culinary virtues of patience, adaptability, and love next to principles like preparation, combination, and procedure. The book hopes to empower cooks in trusting their own intuition and common sense rather than limiting their choices to a voice of authority—the Recipe.

To all you recipe followers out there: May you use what surrounds you, and may you trust what resides within you.

Fare Well.

Why Recipe-Free Cooking?

Why a recipe-free cookbook? Because nobody knows how to cook anymore! Or people hate to cook. Or they don't have the time. Or they don't have the skill. Or they don't have the patience or motivation. Carrie Bradshaw pegged it: "My oven is where I store my sweaters." Those who do cook are bored. Confined to comfort and convenience, they cook the *same ol' same ol'* every week. They don't know how to cook what they like to eat. When people do cook, they rely on cookbooks. They sigh, "If I could just find a book with some good recipes . . ." as if the *right* recipes will teach them how to cook.

People search for that *right* cookbook. They find books with recipes from exotic lands or quaint down-home areas. They look at the pictures of delectable dishes and imagine these dishes prepared for Saturday night's dinner party. They read the recipe names—so interesting and unique—and imagine these dishes delighting friends and family. They purchase expensive specialty foods that sit in pantries and grow mold in refrigerators. Cookbooks silently grow dust on kitchen shelves.

The illusion is that cookbooks propel us into being the type of person we wish to be. We buy vegetarian cookbooks hoping to become vegetarians. We buy Indian cookbooks, craving exotic lifestyles. People buy cookbooks and think that these books will somehow teach them how to cook. Instead, the books are discarded upon a shelf, offering visual validation that we are the books we own. Cookbooks are rarely touched again, except for the random visitor who picks up the dusty book, acknowledges it, and rekindles our desire for buying it in the first place. This person's interest only serves as a sorry reminder that the cookbook is seldom, if ever, used. We blame our dusty cookbooks for not solving our cooking dilemma. Then comes the guilt and shame, which leads to more cookbook buying. We buy more cookbooks to offset the boredom and denial. The solution is that we need a *newer and better* cookbook.

Every cookbook offers good recipes. Recipes are scrutinized, analyzed, tested, revised,

> *Cooking is not about knowing how to follow perfect recipes. Cooking is about knowing how to cook.*

and perfected. Cooking is not about knowing how to follow perfect recipes. **Cooking is about knowing how to cook**. Following a perfect recipe still chains one to a recipe, and this is where our frustration emerges. I think that, intuitively, we understand this. That is why cookbooks gather more dust than use.

People may learn how to follow a few recipes, but they may never learn how to cook. Families no longer teach that. Cultures have dispersed. Meal time is dissipated and diluted. Few have the luxury of time or money to experiment with food and cultivate skills. Creativity is limited to a cookbook's decisions and instructions versus one's intuitive culinary sense. What people feel in their hearts and guts is dispelled by mandated ingredients. Personal taste, local agriculture, seasonality, lifestyle . . . it's all dismissed and replaced by the Recipe Paradigm.

Cooking, nourishing, and heck, *living* is not about finding the perfect recipes. It's about understanding the basic principles. It's about understanding why cooking is so important for maintaining a healthy lifestyle and supporting a healthy environment. It's about understanding that cooking is more than consuming. It is about sustaining—sustaining oneself, one's family, and one's community. Cooking is an intentional interaction between you and your environment. It is an appreciation of our appetites—a celebration for the soul and tummy.

How do we revive cooking? We begin by saying yes. We being by appreciating what cooking has to offer. We see cooking as a wise investment, versus a waste of time. We learn about the holistic benefits of cooking: how it calms our mind, soothes our soul, and improves our health. We embrace the economics of cooking: how it saves money, reduces waste, and instills an adaptable efficiency. We learn that cooking is easy: Once we have the basic tools, we are empowered to nourish ourselves. We begin to care about all of this, and as we do, we become more aware and connected. We learn to nurture and love through food, not just frantically feed the family through empty calories in transit between activities and obligations. Embracing cooking is a mind shift and a behavioral leap. And, it is possible.

While cooking is all these things, recipe-free cooking is all this, plus something more. It is about exploring the moment when you listen to yourself—a sweet, subtle, yet subversive act. What happens when you listen to your own tastes and preferences instead of what some recipe dictates to you? What happens when you invite common sense into your kitchen rather than using procedures that are unhealthy and outdated? What happens when you take into account what thrives in your region, what is fresh and available, and what happens to be in the refrigerator that needs to be used up?

The Vegetarian Chef offers the basics—basic philosophies, procedures, and ingredients—in short, the basic principles. Once we understand the principles, we are free to develop our own recipes.

Give people a recipe, and

they eat tonight.

Teach them how to cook, and

they are nourished for the rest of their lives.

Let's Get Cooking

The objective of cooking is to:

Prepare food in a way that complements nature's original product (to say improves would be committing hubris).

Make food palatable and suitable to our systems (as opposed to processed and unfit for digestion).

Recycle the waste in proper ways, ensuring that we put back into the earth as much as we take from it.

Cooking is art. It unites common sense, intuition, and creativity. Cooking nourishes the creative palate as eating nourishes the culinary palate.

One example is Japanese Culinary Arts.
A Japanese meal
Simple and elegant sculpture
Each bite a haiku

French cuisine also illustrates art. Here, again, preparation and presentation are key elements to a satisfying meal. Perhaps less delicate or structured than Japanese cuisine, French cuisine flows and sings in warm rhythm.

Creating the food is an integral part of the feeding process; it's not merely slapping things together and stuffing one's face. My husband jokes about the American male who eats over the sink. This is far from a joke these days. People eat over the sink, at work cubicles, on the phone, and in front of steering wheels. Eating is a type of invisible unconscious chore that must be dealt without interrupting our productivity. Frank Perdue had disturbing comments to say about raising chickens. He lamented that the problem with raising chickens was that they are living creatures. It is cumbersome, wasting time and money, having to deal with all that *aliveness*.

Cooking and eating are at the core of our existence, yet they're too often ignored in our modern day. Americans tend to eat for comfort and consolation, not due to hunger or necessity. They eat at a hurried pace in frenzied atmospheres. They buy processed food and avoid the kitchen. Eating and cooking have taken on a stigma in our society. They are cumbersome processes designed to interrupt our workflow. Every minute spent eating or cooking is a minute that *could* and *should* be spent making money. Cooking is no longer a part of our culture; it is a luxurious hobby. Some consider cooking indulgent, and some caustic people consider it inferior and submissive. A parent who spends time cooking is an archaic homebody who could be out there in the *real* world earning a living with a career—*really* providing for the family.

This is the fallacy—that cooking is expendable. Cooking is as integral to our health as eating. Cooking touches so many parts of our lives. Cooking is not buying strawberries in February but, rather, picking them fresh in June. Cooking is not eating pizza when sick. It is brewing a steamy pot of soup—or better yet—being nurtured with a pot of soup from a dear friend. Cooking is not opening a bag of cookies when a child comes home from school; it is preparing a batch with them from scratch. Cooking slows us down and consumes our time, in good ways.

Cooking is math, science, reading, history, economics, nutrition, exercise, poetry and art, all rolled into one. Cooking is a multisensory experience: smelling, hearing, seeing, and even touching the food. For you special needs folks, it stimulates executive functioning, social pragmatics, and sensory integration. You want a rich learning experience for your children? You want *quality time* with your family? Cook!

Cooking is a multisensory experience: smelling, hearing, seeing, and even touching the food.

And Eating? Eating is feeding! It nourishes our bodies and satisfies our minds. Eating sustains life and regenerates every cell in our bodies.

An old Yankee adage states, "Wood heats three times: splitting, stacking, and burning." A similar concept applies to food. Food nourishes four ways: preparing, presenting, eating, and digesting.

Digestion begins before the first bite of food enters the mouth. We are physiologically programmed to release necessary digestive enzymes into our intestinal tracts in preparation for digestion, much like the pit crew entering a race track. Normally, this happens naturally, if eating when we are truly hungry, and in a relaxed state and environment. Cooking also initiates the digestive process, by stimulating the flow of digestive juices. Without this necessary step, we may lose much of food's nutritional value. It would be like eating half of the food that you are actually eating—or in more practical terms, throwing away 50% of your food.

It is vital to listen to our bodies for digestion to be efficient and complete. If we do not properly stimulate the digestive process, we won't digest our food. It is as simple as that. Since the time to stimulate the digestive process is *before* eating, this crucial preliminary step must not be eliminated. In these modern times, people have forsaken this delicate process. In the land of Crazybusy, we have alienated ourselves from our own digestion and, in larger ways, our health.

What does Crazybusy tell us about how people are digesting their food? Or about the nutrients we are extracting from our food or the nutrients we are assimilating into our bodies? What does it say about metabolism, anabolism, and catabolism—the chemical processes that feed cells, replace dead cells with new, healthy cells, and supply a constant source of energy to sustain life? What does this say about the quality of health and life in general? A lot. It would take another book to discuss it properly.

Besides, you didn't come here to be lectured. You came here to cook.

So, let's get cooking.

THE BASIC
PHILOSOPHIES

THE BASIC PHILOSOPHIES

Mise en Place

In culinary school, a phrase was drilled into our heads:

MISE EN PLACE.

It was the first thing we learned, on the first day, in the first five minutes of class. The phrase was our axiom and our entire method of cooking. Translated from French, *mise en place* (pronounced *mees en plas*) means, "everything in its place." *Mise en place* is an attitude. It is a process. *Mise en place* was our religion, and we prayed daily.

Mise en place *is a way of being*:

> Take the time to collect your thoughts.
>
> Think about the dish that is to be prepared.
>
> Write down what you are going to cook.
>
> Create lists: list the ingredients, list the utensils and appliances, and list the amount of time needed to create the recipe.
>
> Prepare ingredients before actually cooking.
>
> Have everything at hand, within reach, and ready to use.

Watch any cooking show on television and observe *mise en place*. All food items are cut neatly and placed tidily in glass bowls. Every utensil and appliance is on the counter or stove. As the chefs proceed through the recipe, they methodically pour the contents of these bowls into containers, pots, and pans. All their utensils are within reach, so the chef is able to stand in one place, rather than run around the kitchen searching for the right tool. Everything has a rhythm and flows. Professional chefs make it look so simple; they are conductors in a culinary symphony.

The fact is that cooking *is* simple when there is *mise en place.* (Television chefs even have a lovely finished product waiting to be presented at the end of the show. Wouldn't it be nice to cook for dinner guests, knowing that a perfect meal was already prepared in the oven?)

How do I know the ingredients if I'm not using a recipe?

This is explained in the next section, *The Basic Ingredients.* I offer ideas to get you started. Continue to use past meals and recipes for inspiration and remember to FARE WELL.

Why do I list utensils and appliances?

Mainly, to make sure you have them! Many times I have mixed up a batch of muffins or cake batter, only to find that I do not have the tins or pans to cook them in. A recipe might also suggest using some outmoded item like a potato ricer to make mashed potatoes.

This could be prevented if you identify which items you need and are available, before you begin cooking. (A list of basic utensils and appliances is included to get you started.) Review the procedure and write down utensils or appliances you'll need. Identify things that you don't have, and then problem-solve. For instance, you may not have a loaf pan to make muffins. As your cooking confidence develops, you may be comfortable in easing up on listing everything. But if you are new to the kitchen, be proactive.

Utensils

You keep stressing cooking time. Any special reason?

Cooking time is crucial. Nowadays with the Crazybusy, you need to plan things carefully, often down to minutes.

Let's say you have two hours to prepare dinner. You'll need to be aware of this before you start cooking and prepare something that will be ready in time. Coming home at 6:00 P.M. after a soccer game is not the time to whip up Pot Roast. It is another aspect of being aware in the kitchen, so that everything runs smoothly. This way, you'll enjoy the cooking process by reducing stress. Take advantage of the power of planning ahead; it is rewarding and relaxing.

Mise en place means knowing what you are creating. Visualize it as you go along. Picture the dish completed and ready to serve, the kitchen is clean, and you—the calm, happy, loving chef—ready to enjoy your meal.

Mise en place relates to a theory called *psycho-cybernetics* (Maxwell Maltz, 1960), an off-shoot of cybernetics, which was originally devised for technology and by mathematician Norbert Weiner:

> Cybernetics appeared such a breakthrough to Maltz because its implication was that achievement was a matter of *choice*. Most important to the dynamic of achieving was the 'what' (the target), rather than the 'how' (the path). The frontal lobes or conscious thinking part of the brain could devise the goal, or create the image of the person you wanted to be, and the subconscious mind would deliver its attainment. The 'set and forget' mechanism of guided missiles would also work for our deepest desires. (www.butler-bowdon.com/psychocybernets)

Psycho-cybernetics gained popularity in the sports world, adopted by coaches to improve athletic performance. The experiment involved basketball players picturing themselves at the free throw line. They visualized sinking 10 shots in a row—nothing but net. The players who could achieve this (and oddly, it's harder than one might think) improved their accuracy.

Cybernetics theory asserts that when one "clearly fixes" upon a target or goal and repeatedly focuses clearly or creates a "constant feedback loop," it sets in motion an "automaticity" that self-propels the fixation into fruition. This theory eventually found its way into our psyches and culture, emanating into the self-help genre. Books such as *Do What You Love and the Money Will Follow* and *The Secret* are by-products of cybernetics. Even the recent runaway bestseller, *The Vegetarian Chef*, finds its roots in cybernetics. ;)

Specifically, mise en place ***is to:***

- Have enough time to cook what you are cooking.

- Wash your hands before cooking.

- Wear an apron and drape a dishrag on your apron to keep your hands clean.

- Have a cutting board out. To prevent the board from slipping, place a cloth underneath it.

- Have kitchen towels handy: damp towels for clean-up and a dry towel for wiping hands.

- Bring necessary utensils out and place within reach.

- Preheat the oven.

- Prepare the appliances: Grease a cookie sheet, line cake pan with wax paper, dig out the soup pot, make sure all the pressure cooker parts are together, find all the cords, and wash dirty pans you will be using.

- Prepare all the ingredients: washed, peeled, cut and ready to use.

- Keep your area clean! Fill a bowl or the sink with soapy water. Wash dishes as you go, preventing accumulation of messy stacks.

- Have dish rags on hand to wipe counters and cutting boards as you cook. Use rags to wipe your hands, and keep a separate rag on the counter for wiping.

I once worked for a chef (Chef Pierre—more on him soon) who had a unique strategy for developing *mise en place* sensibilities. If I didn't know where something was in the kitchen, I would ask him, and he would reply, "Ten bucks if I find it." If he had to stop what he was doing to waste his time looking for something that I should be able to find—*and then found it*—he would deduct $10 from my paycheck.

At first I thought he was being a tyrant, but he did teach me to look *thoroughly* before asking for help. Ninety percent of the time, I would find what I was looking for. It just took an iota of patience and perseverance (with a dollop of self-reliance). Nowadays, when husband and sons ask me where their socks or wallets or ski hats are, I remember Chef Pierre and bark back, "Ten bucks if I find it!"

❦   ❦   ❦

Most importantly, *mise en place* involves cooking with seven ingredients found in every single recipe . . .

Seven Virtues of Cooking

COMMON SENSE   CLEANLINESS

IMAGINATION   PATIENCE

INTUITION   LOVE

CONSERVATION

These virtues are the most important ingredients in all cooking. Always have plenty of these on hand. Place the list on your refrigerator. Keep them well stocked in your pantry. Give them freely, when your neighbors run out!

COMMON SENSE 🐛

Common sense involves *mise en place*, plus a bit more. It involves thinking through the cooking process—from beginning to end—and making sure you have the knowledge, ingredients, and time to cook the dish. Sounds simple? It is and it isn't. Before you begin to cook anything, ask yourself:

1. **WHAT AM I MAKING?**

2. **WHAT INGREDIENTS ARE NECESSARY?**

3. **WHAT INGREDIENTS ARE ACCESSORY?**

4. **DO I UNDERSTAND THE PROCESS?**

1. What am I making?

This is key. You might compare this question to a centering or visualizing activity.

Think about what you are making and why you are making it. Picture it: the textures, colors, and flavors. Are you making soup? Imagine arriving home one chilly winter afternoon from a long walk. Your cold fingers and toes ache and throb. Your nose and ears redden and pulse. Your body has stiffened slightly, and your lips are sluggish, making it difficult to speak. Now, picture yourself walking into your home and being greeted by the smell of spicy simmering soup. Feel the hot bowl cradled in your cold hands. Feel the steam rise, swirling, melting your face, and clearing your nose, causing it to run just a little bit. The toasty soup heats your body and rekindles your internal furnace.

Aaah . . . warm, satisfying soup.

Choose foods that make sense. Summertime calls for fresh fruit, cold salads, and iced drinks. Winter is the time for hearty stews and warm baked bread. Oatmeal makes a tummy happy on a cool autumn morning. A heavy meal—pizza, quiche, or fried food—deserves a light dessert.

Mise en place sounds the same as common sense. What's the difference?

The difference is that *mise en place* is the organizational aspect, whereas common sense is the realistic aspect.

One of the first dinner parties I cooked for my family turned out to be one of the worst. The food was tasty. However, I made: Cheddar cheese soup, Quiche Lorraine (Swiss cheese, onion, and bacon), salad with Gorgonzola blue cheese dressing, and cheesecake for dessert. Talk about Dairy Overkill! I cheesed my poor family right off.

I may have organized my meal and had everything in its place while cooking. But I never stopped to think about how each part of the menu related to the whole. Take time before you prepare anything to think about what you are doing. Picture the dish as completed: a steaming pot of stew . . . warm, moist gingerbread . . . a colorful, crisp salad. Notice how the ingredients in the dish complement each other and how each dish complements the meal. If they don't, recruit your common sense. You don't have to make it complicated. Just remember my cheesy meal—and avoid that!

2. What ingredients are necessary?

I emphasize the "necessary" here. Throughout this book, I refer to the "main" or necessary ingredients of your dish. What ingredients are at the core? What ingredients are *so* necessary that the recipe would not *be the recipe* without them?

Take Cream of Cauliflower soup. What ingredients are necessary?

- Cauliflower

- Water

These are the only ingredients needed to make Cream of Cauliflower soup. And really, the only main ingredient is cauliflower. The main ingredient must *count.* It is the foundation. It is the signature of the dish in texture, flavor, or nutrition—ideally, all three. In a way, the main ingredients tell the story of the dish.

Okay, here is the story of cauliflower and water—our main ingredients. Now that isn't much of a soup, is it? This is why there are accessory ingredients.

3. What ingredients are accessory?

They are all the rest! Accessory ingredients are the details of the story, offering flavor, color, texture, and garnish. As they are accessory, they may be substituted as desired.

Accessory ingredients for Cream of Cauliflower soup:

- Onion
- Garlic
- Mellow White Miso
- Cream
- Thickener
- Salt & pepper

These ingredients would make a fine soup. But since they are accessory, they are changeable. This is where *you* enter the kitchen.

Don't like onions? Omit them! Like mushrooms? Add them! Feeding garlic lovers? Add a bunch! How much? Start with a couple cloves, taste, and continue adding a clove at a time, until your soup tastes great! No Mellow White Miso? No problem! There are at least 30 other varieties!

Add tomatoes, leftover squash, chopped turkey, carrots, beans, etc. Make it spicy. Use what is available. Use what you like. You are the CEO—Culinary Executive Officer—of your kitchen.

Accessory ingredients offer the freedom to be creative. They shift thinking in terms of recipes to personal tastes and values, which allow us to make personal choices. Personal choice has a practical side beyond creativity. It allows room for food allergies, intolerance, or sensitivities (which seem to be on the rise in our culture).

4. Do I understand the process?

This remains a major problem for wannabe cooks. They love to be in the kitchen, they love to cook, and they frequently try recipes. One barrier is in understanding cooking procedures. Cooking—like any art or science—comprises its own language. A recipe says to fold in the egg whites. If you do not know how to fold in the egg whites, the egg whites do not get folded in, and the recipe is ruined. This breeds frustration and discouragement for even the most adventurous of cooks.

Cooking processes are covered later, under "The Basic Procedures." You may not be comfortable with some of these procedures. Please remember that this is just a guide and cannot replace experiential learning. Begin here with the basics, and then use those interactive options to learn as much as you want. In this way, you develop your own process and speak your own cooking language.

IMAGINATION 🐖

Often people look at a recipe, find one or two ingredients they do not like, scrunch up their noses and say, "Eeuww . . . I don't like raisins. I'm not making these muffins!"

This is where I'd like to gently throttle my lady who left Marlene's Market and Deli, refusing the 30 miso alternatives. Now is the time for guts and glory! It's time for imagination. Don't like raisins? Omit the raisins! Substitute with something you *do* like. Do you like apricots? Add apricots! How about pineapple and coconut? Walnuts or pecans or dates? Oh, boy!

Miso lady aside, what might be considered the real inspiration for this book began with *Mish Mash*, an improv baking game that I played with my sister Franny. At 3 years old, I spent happy hours making playdough creations. Then, later, my best friend, Arla and I would play Mish Mash, after school. Only seven years old, we'd "bake all by ourselves" (play with ingredients, while my mommy made dinner).

The cool thing about Mish Mash was that, every once in a while, we'd drift from play dough to real dough. My first edible masterpiece was a green pie crust. It had butter, sugar, and flour (and green food coloring). It was cooked. It was edible. (Let's be lenient with the word "edible," shall we?) I was so proud of that rubbery green circle. Without a cookbook or mother dictating my decisions, I created something to eat with my own imagination. I was only 3 years old! If I could do it, so can you.

The key is to be bold while having fun. Experiment and try new things! Use common sense to lead you, but try to imagine flavors that sound interesting and tasty. As a reference, think of what you already like to eat. Then allow your intuition to guide you. Mish Mash!

Remember to laugh in your kitchen. Laugh and enjoy yourself. If you ruin a meal, you'll still nourish yourself with a good story.

It's often easier to think of combinations that go well together than it is to think up some that do not. This sounds odd, until you experiment. When Arla and I Mish Mashed, we discovered how much we understood about cooking, even as naive children. We had a sense of what spices were "baking" spices and what fruits went into baking. We figured that some things would be no-no's, like putting mustard in Banana Bread. But then again, you might surprise yourself when you start challenging assumptions about what goes together and what doesn't.

You might say, *"Well, I wouldn't put hot dogs into muffins."* And, I'd reply, "Oh, really? Ever try Pigs in a Blanket? Or, bacon pancakes? How about Sweet and Sour pork? I remember a recipe for Sweet and Sour sauce that combined jelly with mustard. It sounds icky, but I found it to be quite tasty. You wouldn't put mustard in coffee, right? Well, that might make an interesting *Mole*-type of sauce. Who knows how something might taste, until you experiment?

Look, that's all well and good. But I don't have a million dollars to turn my kitchen into a science lab. And I don't have a million hours of time.

Of course you don't. So honor the first virtue: common sense. When experimenting, try small batches of new recipes (in case that *Mole* sauce tastes more like *Moldy* sauce). Keep it simple and use inexpensive ingredients. Being cautious doesn't exclude being creative. Be a happy chemist and a brave explorer in your kitchen. Have some fun and expect some things to be . . . let's just say, "learning experiences." We are supposed to make mistakes; they offer opportunities to change and grow.

Let us also honor prudence, however. Heed Martha Stewart's tip: Experiment with new recipes on people for whom you do not wish to impress. More simply, don't try new ideas out on company. You may end up with flop for dinner . . . more mash than mish.

When something goes wrong—and it will—all the time—be ready to improvise with your imagination. I adore the scene in *Bridget Jones' Diary* when Bridget cooks her own birthday feast to impress her friends. Although she has no idea how to cook, she has lofty expectations. Brazenly ignoring Martha's tip, Bridget attempts some fancy recipes. Her leek soup turns blue, and her orange *soufflé* transforms into vile marmalade. Bridget's friend Mark (the fabulous Colin Firth) arrives in the nick of time to save the day. As he surveys the culinary war zone, he suggests, "Do you have any eggs?" She does. He smiles and loosens his tie. "Well then, omelets it is."

Remember to laugh in your kitchen. Laugh and enjoy yourself. If you ruin a meal, you'll still nourish yourself with a good story. Trust that you are taking chances, learning to cook, and practicing Top Kitchen Tip # 9 (Observe and Retain). You are also applying Rule # 6 from the great life-opening book, *The Art of Possibility* (Ben & Rosamond Zander). Rule # 6: Don't take yourself so goddamned seriously.

For all you cynics out there, look. I may be dumb, but I'm not stupid. Be prudent with this virtue. I'm not recommending that you buy thousands of dollars' worth of food and then create your own manic Betty Crocker fantasyland. I'm saying, like Martha Beck advises in *Steering by Starlight,* to listen to your intuition and respond to what feels right. Your road to culinary intelligence may be achieved "brick by brick"—in small, manageable, and affordable increments. Or maybe you prefer a more manic approach. Some of us thrill in bashing the walls with sledge hammers: quit jobs, leave husbands, and move to India, all in one month. Heck, it worked out well for Elizabeth Gilbert. With new cooks, I might advise a more "brickly" approach, however. Start with meals and recipes you already enjoy, and change an ingredient or two. Become aware of local foods and include these more regularly. Allow some time and space to be frivolous and free in your kitchen. This uncensored type of cooking often yields surprisingly tasty results.

And when that fails . . . well then, omelets it is.

INTUITION 🐍

Intuition loves to cook. Like a sweet butterfly, it rests upon my shoulder, whispering subtle suggestions. Its soft veil swirls and sings, watching over me. Logic is certainly required in the kitchen. Cooking is serious stuff. After all, we are dealing with fire, chemicals, and bacteria or other possibly fatal organisms! Still, being a great cook—like all art forms—requires a bit of magic. One must listen to one's butterfly if one is to transform.

How does intuition cook? Join me as we shop at our local food co-op. I'm buying some grains. I peruse the bulk bins, allowing my eyes to wander over the different varieties. Eventually, I'll settle on one or two, drawn to them for no particularly logical reason. I may be drawn to the color, shape, or name. I experience this moment as a *Bing*—a positive sensation, sweetly and swiftly emerging in my mind and body. Instead of trying to figure out why, I simply listen and respond. Today the *Bing* is brown basmati rice.

I've made my choice. Next, I need to decide, how much? There are logical ways to determine this. It seems sensible to compute just how much rice is needed for four people eating two portions for three days. I might feel it necessary to determine the length of time between shopping excursions so that I have enough rice to sustain my family until the next trip. If I'm like most people (or if you're like me), by the time I derive these calculations, I'll need to add a bottle of tequila to my shopping list in order to drown out the headache I've developed in figuring out the answer.

> *One must listen to one's butterfly, if one is to transform.*

Besides, logic doesn't take into account the fact that someone will get hungry at 11:00 P.M. and snack on the rice or that I might want to play with some leftover rice and make a pudding, or that our dog may be extra cute and warrant a rice snack, or that friends will drop by and I'll want to offer them some rice for lunch. No, logic does not take any of these unknowns into account. How could it? Logic doesn't know about any of these upcoming events. But there is something that does.

Somehow, some way . . . intuition knows. How does it know? I don't know. I've cooked with intuition for decades now—sheesh, four decades, as I type this! And I can say with confidence that intuition guides me into pouring just the right amount of rice that will supply what I need and even for what I don't yet know that I need. If I allow my body to relax and loosen my mind, breathe and smile, and trust the process, the answers arrive.

The way I decide how much rice to buy is to walk over to the bags and grab a size that I'm drawn to—*Bing*— and begin to fill the bag with rice. *Bing*—I stop when it feels right. I don't think about it; it's a gut response ("Wild" Things chapter). It's more of a positive sensation. Like a Geiger counter, I navigate in the "centered zone": a calm, attentive state. I notice when something feels right. It feels light and flowy and good—a *Bing*. When it feels incorrect or when I'm forcing a decision, I can feel the "no." It feels duller, heavier, and grey—more like a *Thud*.

I'm impressed by how accurate intuition is as a guide. When I return home and refill my glass rice jar, the bag of rice reaches the top. How did I know how much to get? I don't know. I just did. Thank you, Intuition. You rock. No, dude, you *Bing*.

Intuition is a skill and needs to be practiced like any skill in order to refine and develop. I didn't have this ability as a young girl making Mish Mash. But after years of cooking, it is second nature. I have developed an ability to recognize the messages. Like any message, I can choose to ignore it. And when I do . . . well, the results are definitely more *Thud* than *Bing*.

CONSERVATION

Fresh out of culinary school, I found myself working in Florida at an intimate French bistro called Café du Parc. The proprietors, Pierre and Ann Marie Latuberne, moved from their small village in France to southern Florida, where they offered their local delicacies created in the traditional style. This was *classic* French cuisine, and I was one of only two *sous chefs* (assistants to the head chef) in the kitchen. It was a fantastic gig procured by the infamous Chef Henin (whom you will hear about, in just a bit).

One day, I was preparing carrots for a stew. The first part of preparing them was to cut off the ends. I cut about an inch off the fat end of each carrot. Chef Pierre approached me and glared at the inch-long stubs. I stopped cutting and stood there with knife in hand. Fixing his gaze directly at me, he grabbed my free hand and turned it over, palm side up.

"This is your raise in six months," he said, picking up one of the carrot stubs and placing it in my hand. He picked up another stub.

"This is your Christmas bonus." He placed the second stub next to the first.

"And this." He held the third stub in front of my eyes. "This is your week's paid vacation at the end of your first year."

With the three carrot stubs in my hand, he waited, the glare unwavering. I looked down at the stubs and then at him.

"GOT IT?" he demanded.

"I got it, Chef." I replied, meekly.

"Good." He walked away.

Do *you* get it? I wasted the ends of those carrots needlessly! I could have saved food, time, and money by using the whole carrot. These things add up quickly. Conserving is more efficient, and that is what you are becoming.

In culinary school, most of the production kitchens had about three bags of garbage at the end of their shifts. One chef stood out. His kitchen created a mere half-bag of garbage. Master Chef Roland Henin was a master of conservation. Arguably, he enjoyed his reputation as the finest yet meanest chef of the Culinary Institute of America. Students openly feared and secretly revered him. Chef Henin taught the "PM" shift, meaning the dinner shift. Classes would rotate every month into a new unit. So every month, Chef Henin would have a new group of students. At the beginning of the unit, he would announce that if the group's performance was particularly outstanding, they could stay after class to ask him questions. Now, "after class" is around midnight, so the last thing any young alcohol-driven culinary student wants is to "have the honor" of staying after class to ask questions—questions that wouldn't even be on a future test!

Except . . .

Except that this was *Master Chef Roland Henin.* Everyone knew it was a rare honor to speak with this great man and that, in turn, offered bragging rights: *The later we stayed, the better we looked.* Culinary school was competitive, and we used every possible marker available to distinguish ourselves from our peers, in order to gain the prime opportunities, come postgraduation. In the evenings, as other classes were ending their PM shifts, you could hear students milling down the halls and heading for the bars. Everyone would take a moment to peek into Chef Henin's kitchen. If the lights were still on, they'd stare jealously at the sacred group who had performed an exemplary job and were duly awarded the privilege of remaining in the presence of the Great One to garner sage secrets of the craft.

One night, our group held the honors. I remember seeing my friends walk by, peeking into the kitchen windows, trying to get a look at who made the grade. I swelled with pride while trying to focus on whatever the heck it was we were talking about in our kitchen, happily distracted by the attention we were getting in the hallway.

Actually, we were all a bit stunned to find ourselves here. We stood frozen and mute. Chef Henin started asking the questions.

"What ees zee definition of cooking?"

The group quickly scanned each other, trying to see if our eyes could reveal the answer he was seeking. A brave student initiated.

"Cooking is . . . the art . . . of food preparation?"

"Ees zat an answer or a question?"

"An . . . answer, Chef?"

"Zat ees another question, and the answer to both ees *NO*."

A few more dared to guess.

"Cooking is culinary art?"

"No."

"Cooking is the act of changing food to create a more palatable form?"

"No."

Then the contrived answers came.

"Cooking is the craft of the palate."

"Cooking is a dance—the fusion of food, movement, heat, and soul."

"Cooking is the human's way of agricultural manipulation."

"Cooking is a form of gastronomic physics."

No, no, no . . . *What?*

Each of us expelled an answer that was vaguely correct but mostly a pathetic attempt to impress and entertain the Great One. The last student offered the final inaccurate answer. Chef Henin grew quiet and looked down. He walked over to the garbage can and extracted a discarded salmon carcass. He held it up and waved it in front of everyone's face as he proclaimed:

"Cooking ees *soufflé* from sheet. Eet is taking zee dried-up, deescarded carcahss and creating ahn eleegahnt feeszh terrine. Eet ees taking zee scraps of vegetables and tahrning them into *brunoises* (tiny diced vegetables) and flavorful *consommé*.

Eet ees not stahnding around on yahr aahz waiting for zee yeeahr-old, organeek, graahz-fehd veeyal to arriahve from New Zeahlahnd. Inywaahn kahn maayk *Veeyal Marsala* from tender veeyal. But to make an eksqueezeet *Zalmahn Croquette* from sheety pieces of leftovahr carcahss and ahging vegetables in zee refrigerator: Now, *zees* ees cooking. Never forget zees. Zee rehst ees bullsheet. *Shoemaker* sheet."

Master Chef Roland Henin's definition of cooking?

Scraps equals Soufflé

Anyone can take quality ingredients and create a masterpiece. A true chef integrates the art of conservation.

Conservation is utilizing as much as possible: removing only the tip of the carrot, utilizing turnip and beet greens, recreating leftovers, making stock from so-called vegetable waste, and composting the unusable food remains. It is of dire urgency that we conserve and sustain our resources in all aspects of our life. When we conserve in the kitchen, we gingerly reinforce this practice.

CLEANLINESS ❧

A clean kitchen is an efficient kitchen. Everything is easy to find. Cooking takes less time. Thoughts are organized. A clutter-free kitchen creates visual-spatial serenity. There's less chance for contamination and food poisoning—a legitimate concern in any kitchen. Clean-up is swifter and less stressful.

Wise steps to follow for cleanliness:

1. **START WITH A CLEAN KITCHEN.**
2. **CLEAN WHILE YOU COOK.**
3. **CLEAN UP AFTER COOKING.**

1. Start with a clean kitchen.
You are more likely to cook if you have a clean kitchen, and cooking will take less time.

2. Clean while you cook.

- Put ingredients away after use.
- Fill a bowl with hot water.

- Rinse used dishes that aren't "dirty"—bowls that held raw vegetables, for instance.

- Keep a soapy sponge handy for dirty dishes.

- Wash dishes as you go along. Food won't stick, and you'll use less water.

- Put large, bulky appliances like blenders and food processors away after cleaning. (Reassemble these appliances so they're ready to use again.)

In 1984, I cooked at the Century Plaza, in Los Angeles (the year L.A. hosted the summer Olympics). An intern from the Culinary Institute of America, I was still an eager and naïve cook. I worked as a Floater: subbing for people's days off, covering meal breaks, and supporting busy sections. On this particular day, my job involved handling the menu for the employee cafeteria. It entailed cooking 200 portions of 2 different entrees, plus *starch and veg* (potatoes and vegetables).

I chose barbecued chicken for an entree. I recall making the sauce and placing the chicken onto several sheet pans (long, rectangular pans, used for baking large quantities). Next I began to dole out the sauce. I splashed ladles filled with barbecue sauce all over the chicken, the counter, and myself.

I rushed and hurried, wanting to do a good job. I figured that since I was working so productively, I was supposed to get messy. Wiping barbecue sauce off my cheek, I smiled, self-satisfied.

At that moment, Executive Chef Raymond Hoffmeister passed by my station. He noticed my frantic endeavors. As he approached me, he stopped abruptly and cried out, "What has happened to you?!"

A little shocked, I replied, "Uh, Chef, I'm making barbecued chicken for the cafeteria lunch."

He stared at my workstation and at my uniform, shook his head angrily, and in the most controlled screaming voice, addressed me.

"How-can-you-accomplish-*anything*-this-way? What a mess! Don't you have pride in your work? I'd be *ashamed* to work this way! I'm ashamed to have to look at this mess." He whispered the last sentence sternly in my ear. "You are a disgrace to my kitchen." He left me with my foolish pride, now as soiled as my uniform.

I learned the value of cleanliness from Chef Hoffmeister. Organize your mind before you step into a kitchen. Organize your kitchen before you begin to cook. Be proud of what you do and how you are doing it . . .
. . . and a messy cook isn't necessarily a good cook!

3. Clean up after cooking.

- While things are baking and simmering, clean up.

- When the food is ready, so is the kitchen. You'll have room to prepare the food for serving, and you'll avoid a messy kitchen when you bring the dirty dishes in after supper.

To sum up cleanliness, heed Chef Pierre's sage advice: You got time to lean, you got time to clean!

PATIENCE ?

Haste makes waste. How many meals have you ruined due to mismanaging time and then rushing around frantically in the kitchen? How much time is wasted due to racing around a store and then forgetting to buy certain ingredients? I'm no saint. I've done these enough times to nominate patience as a virtue in cooking.

Patience invites you to *notice* the creative adventure of cooking. Breathe deeply and calm down. This does not suggest moving sluggishly and ineffectively. Some people feel more fluid moving at a faster pace and this is fine. Fast or slow, by *relaxing* into the pace, you accomplish far more. Ask any monk interested in neuroscience about flow: When we meditate, our brainwaves shift into an alpha state instead of our typically frenzied beta state. In this meditative alpha state—or what Herbert Bensen of the Mind-Body Institute at Harvard calls *The Relaxation Response*—we are able to see more clearly, in a more diffused and broad perspective. Relaxing ignites our ability to problem-solve; we literally and figuratively have the capacity to see more. Relaxation creates a state of heightened awareness, which encourages adaptability and efficiency. Ironically, what our crazybusy society really needs, in order to be more productive, is to be less productive. Or, to be more productive, we need to be more relaxed. We must value both mental states equally.

Remember the *Bing*? Intuition runs on alpha power, baby. It's kind of like our visual spectrum. Some light waves are indiscernible to our naked eye. Literally, some things we cannot see, due to their wavelength. We need to be engaged in the appropriate mental state to receive and perceive intuitive information—so we can see it, in a sense.

In his memoir *Kitchen Confidential*, Chef Anthony Bourdain describes the ambience of Chef Eric Ripert's kitchen in New York City's famed restaurant, Le Bernardin. To say that things run smoothly in Ripert's kitchen is the Mount Vesuvius of understatements. Absent are the stereotypical roles of Head Chef and his minion underlings. The pace flows steadily and coordinated. All sounds reflect synchronized cooking: sautéing, broiling, whisking, and boiling. Absent is the chaos: pans crashing, people shrieking, and anger mounting. If you were to enter the kitchen, you would hear lyrical collaboration instead of staccato profanity. Visually, there is flow as well: People slide back and forth, in between, under and through each other, and around the equipment. Movement is intentional and precise and never wasted. Words, movements, and behaviors are thought out and proactive. In fact, if you were to enter the kitchen at Le Bernardin, you might not have any idea of the level of intensity and advanced culinary expertise to which you were witnessing. This might be the greatest compliment of all. The mark of any expert is in exhibiting his craft to his audience with such grace and innate ability that it seems effortless. This is the magic. It simply appears so easy to the untrained eye.

Relaxing ignites our ability to problem-solve; we literally and figuratively have the capacity to see more.

Chef Eric Ripert is an icon of patience. He understands that the key to an impeccably-run, three-star Michelin restaurant is in the conductor. (The Michelin guide is recognized as the most acclaimed rating system, with three stars being the highest rating.) He must set the tone and model this tone at every moment. He *is* the tone. He is the *Bing*.

We need to be engaged in the appropriate mental state to receive and perceive intuitive information—so we can see it, in a sense.

Even in our less god-like kitchens, patience is essential. Patience is adaptability and resiliency—in other words, tolerance. If at the last minute an Indian stew needs to become an Italian stew because you're out of curry powder, patience allows the smooth improvisation. Patience will see you through any last minute changes: more guests for dinner, a burnt roast, your dog eating freshly-baked rolls, or a cheesecake that takes an extra 90 minutes to bake (they are known to do that). Patience helps you when your child "helps you" in the kitchen. It persists with you when you don't want to cook and must.

LOVE 🐾

When Sammy was born, I asked my midwife how many times a day he would nurse. She replied, "About 50." I thought, *What the hell is she talking about? He'd be eating constantly (and I'd be nursing constantly . . .)! What am I, an IV? She must've said 15.*

She didn't. She said 50. And she was right; eat constantly, he did. Well, nurse constantly. As an infant, he relied on me as his sole (soul) nourishment, and nursing was the way he received it: food, touch, comfort, connection, communication . . . in short, love.

Now we know about the "love drug," *oxytocin*—a neurochemical that is released during nursing, which promotes bonding and builds the immune system. Nursing also stimulates NGF—Neural Growth Hormone—which initiates brain cell growth or *neurogenesis*, regulates hormonal function, and repairs damaged or aged cells. Science understands how we nourish with more than just nutrients. At the time, all I knew is that . . .

this child needed to eat love more than he needed to eat food.

The most valuable ingredient in the kitchen is the rarest. Cooking *needs* love. Without it, cooking is a job, a thankless chore that merely wastes one's time. With love, cooking is a ceremony, an act of concern and affection. Cooking becomes an art and a pleasure. It is not only cooking that needs love. Eating is another lost art that used to be as much about gathering and sharing as consuming. Eating has taken on a more robotic and dismissive quality these days. *"Fast food, on-the-go, grab 'n' gulp, in-and-out, convenience"*—these are the phrases that describe our relationship to eating. Our bad.

Eating is nourishing, rebuilding, and rejuvenating. An image that sustains me is the European meal. Picture an Italian or French family gathering outside at a long wooden table with simple white linen. Trees surround the garden, kids run around the yard, people laugh and relax. Wine is poured, bread is broken, and toasts are made. Laughter is as much a part of the meal as the food itself.

Cooking and eating with love offer a twist: "You are HOW you eat."

Communal meals have earned praise by people who encourage quality time with family. Eating with others initiates conversation, resulting in slower eating. It's a matter of parallel processing: One cannot chew, swallow, talk, and breathe at the same time (or one shouldn't if one wants to avoid choking).

Psychology Today published an article, "A Palate for Pleasure," (Jan/Feb, 2012), claiming, "Enjoyment of food affects the nutritional value of the food; the greater the pleasure, the more nutrients are absorbed." Enjoyment of one's meal initiates specific chemical releases that elevate mood, stimulate digestion, and promote immune health. I like to think of this as a modification to the saying, "You are what you eat." Cooking and eating with love offer a twist: "You are HOW you eat."

Reflecting on Masaru Emoto's fantastic discoveries in *The Hidden Messages in Water,* we observe how thoughts transmit energy waves that may affect water crystal formation, both positively and negatively. The profound influence on negative messages significantly deranged the crystals, whereas compassionate messages, such as "Thank you" and "I love you," produced symmetric, clear, and lovely crystals.

Eating in community offers another benefit. Eating slowly allows the hypothalamus—the part of the brain responsible for controlling our appetite—to signal that we are satiated. It takes the hypothalamus about 20 minutes to initiate the chemical reaction necessary to deliver the signal. Crazybusy eating pays no mind to the meal or the hypothalamus. Unaware and hurried, focusing on our next appointment or surfing through our phones, we ignore its signal. That translates into overeating, which leads to indigestion and obesity. The simple act of eating with others in a relaxed pace can elevate and sustain one's health. Beautiful. I love when health can be so logical.

My dear sister-in-law once prepared a meal for the family. She's not much for the kitchen. Knowing my background in culinary arts, she asked me to comment on the meal. She and I embrace a candid relationship. I replied, "I can taste the Hate." It may sound weird, but you *can* taste the love or hate in food. Pay attention to your next meal. See if you notice this.

When you cook with love, you give love. It is simply an extension of caring for your friends and family. Food nourishes in many ways: physically, emotionally, and spiritually. Cooking with love nourishes all three.

More and more, science and spirituality are joining hands and singing *Kumbaya* in rapt agreement: Thoughts and intentions move waves, forming and flowing particles, which in turn, create our realities. Our thoughts and feelings affect our physical world. If you cook with love, you provide nourishment to the meal and everyone who eats it. That includes you, dear.

Let your cooking delight you. Cook for family and friends. Be grateful for the act of cooking, that you have the power to create edible works of art for your loved ones. If you live alone, "loved ones" are you and your spirit. Be intentional and grateful in your kitchen. Smile and enjoy yourself. You and your loved ones (and the food!) will appreciate the change of heart.

Cook with love and you infuse love into your food. You ingest love, you digest and assimilate love.

How cool is that?

Top Ten Tips in the Kitchen

1. FARE WELL	6. COOK SAFELY
2. KISS	7. RESPECT THE COMFORT ZONE
3. PRECOOK	8. COOKING = HEALTH
4. COOKING IS AN ART	9. OBSERVE AND RETAIN
5. COOK WISELY	10. COOK FOOD UNTIL IT IS DONE

1. FARE WELL

FARE WELL = Fresh, Ripe, Whole, and Local

The best foods FARE WELL: Fresh, Ripe, Whole and Local. These are the most valuable foods in terms of nutrient density and often the best tasting. "Fresh, ripe, and whole" typically mean raw or unprocessed: fruits, vegetables, nuts, sprouts, and fresh juices. Raw foods contain live enzymes, which aid in digestion. Include these foods in your diet regularly.

Shopping at local farm stands, farmer's markets, and natural foods stores (and sections in traditional supermarkets) are your best bets. They provide food that thrives in your geographical area. Fresh ripe foods provide the most nutrition and flavor. Whole foods provide optimal nutrition, due to minimal processing and refinement. Buying locally supports your neighbors, stimulates local economy, and saves on fuel costs—all reducing your carbon footprint.

If you don't want to save the planet, save yourself. FARE WELL provides you with the richest health benefits. To understand the value in nutrient density, I offer this metaphor to my students.

Let's refer to it as the *Paycheck Principle*: Say you work some job for 40 hours a week. At the end of the week, your boss approaches you with two paycheck options: one is a check for $1,000.00; the other one is a check for $50.00. Which check

Why get paid in $50.00 of nutrition for all your effort, when you can get paid $1,000.00?

would you take for your work? I hope you said $1,000.00. Please tell me you did. That wasn't a trick question.

It's the same thing with cooking. Your job is to shop, prepare, eat, digest, and excrete your food. Why not get every single nutritional penny that's coming to you?

2. KISS

Keep Ingredients Simple, Sweetheart. When seasoning with herbs and spices, use around three . . . ish. Too many ingredients confuse and complicate the flavor of a dish and distract from the main ingredients. There will be exceptions. I don't generally count salt and pepper as spices. Mole and curry rely on many flavors. However, as you learn to cook, limiting herbs and spices allows the flavor of FARE WELL to burst through. This is illustrated in fine dining. The awesomeness of the main ingredients makes the dish, rather than doctoring it up with a slew of seasonings. One of the best salads is made simply with fresh vine-ripened tomatoes, fresh mozzarella, and fresh basil, drizzled with extra-virgin olive oil, aged balsamic vinegar, and coarsely ground salt and pepper—fantastic!

3. PRECOOK

Precooking is a major part of *mise en place*. It motivates you to cook and keeps your kitchen in control. Precooking involves:

- ✔ Thawing food
- ✔ Washing and cutting vegetables
- ✔ Preparing dressings
- ✔ Rinsing sprouts
- ✔ Soaking and/or cooking beans
- ✔ Cooking grains
- ✔ Creating marinades
- ✔ Marinating food

Prepare vegetables perpetually. If you have vegetables washed, cut, and ready to cook or eat, then you will. How many times have we bought vegetables, tucked them into the crisper, and discovered the poor things days later, rotted and slimy? I've *86*ed so much food, it's ridiculous. Stop wasting food and money! Good intentions seldom nourish a body; rather, they spoil the mind with guilt.

Hold up. 86ed?

Oh, yes. **"86" is an industry term for getting rid of spoiled food or running out of a food item.** When chefs say, "*86* the veal!" they mean: "Excuse me. Might I have your attention for a brief moment? We are out of the veal entrée. Inform your customers, please." Or they might mean: "Oh, goodness. The rats seem to have beaten us to the veal. Therefore, we are no longer serving it. Inform your customers, please."

Professional kitchens have *86* boards where said items are listed. An *86* board is a type of shopping list, reminding us of what we are out of and need to replace. Professional kitchens rely on *86* boards to create their *mise en place* for the next day's production.

Mornings and weekends are great times to precook, but again, follow your own rhythm. You will need less time and be more prepared (and relaxed) later. Precooking is like having a *sous* chef. In fact, have more than one sous chef; get the kids involved with precooking. It doesn't take a college degree to soak beans or peel carrots. Giddyup!

4. COOKNG IS AN ART

Few art methodologies can compare to the whimsy and practicality of the culinary medium.

It's called culinary arts for a reason. There is a creative process and product involved in cooking. Some people love the process of making art. Some people love the product. Cooking rocks, as it emphasizes both! Cooking is satisfying to the artist who loves possibilities *and* the craftsman who respects decisiveness. Cooking is both art and craft—plus, it's a life skill! Few art methodologies can compare to the whimsy and practicality of the culinary medium.

When cooking, remember the artistic lens. Consider color combinations, textures, and shapes. Consider the "bite-ability" of the dish. You don't want a huge chunk of carrot obstructing a sweet forkful of melodic bean and rice salad. Cut your accessory ingredients into shapes that complement the main ingredients, such as long veggie strips for Angel Hair pasta, tidy bits for burritos, and paper-thin slices for your sandwich fixins. Think of your dish as a work of art, and respect the visual-spatial nature of your piece. Make the appearance pretty and the structure logical—with complementary sizes and shapes—for symbiotic chewing.

5. COOK WISELY

Reduce, reuse, and recycle. Remember the virtue of conservation? Modern times call for sustainable measures. Follow Master Chef Roland Henin's axiom: Scraps equals *Soufflé*!

Reuse cooking liquid in other dishes. While some nutrients are destroyed by cooking, some leech into the cooking liquid. Reserve the liquid from steaming vegetables, soaking seaweed, or reconstituting dried mushrooms. These liquids provide a simple vegetable stock. When liquid is needed for a stew or soup, stock adds nutrients and flavor. Use this stock in bread making and in cooking grains and beans. Drink it as a nutritious broth, give it to your pets, and water your plants!

Recycling in the kitchen goes beyond # 2 plastic containers. Recycle your food, too! Use leftovers in breads, salads, and stews. Ever notice how a restaurant will have fresh broccoli as a side dish on Monday and Tuesday, then Cream of Broccoli soup on Wednesday? Today's main dish is tomorrow's recreation. It's why you see steak sandwiches for Saturday's lunch after Friday night's Prime Rib special or seafood crepes for Sunday brunch, after the weekend's Catch of the Day. Restaurants cook wisely to reduce waste and increase profit, and so should you.

NOTE: "Product" is a general culinary term referring to food items. It might be individual items in a dish or the finished whole dish.

6. COOK SAFELY

Avoid storing cooked or perishable protein between 45°–140°F for more than an hour. Basically, think of it this way: Any protein product—dairy, meat, eggs, tofu, etc.—contains bacteria, and your kitchen is one gigantic petri dish. Many bacteria are beneficial, but some are detrimental. Good or bad, most will begin reproducing in this range.

When in doubt, avoid room temperature. Store perishable food items in the refrigerator. After cooked food has cooled off, wrap and place in the refrigerator. Keep your proteins in the fridge or keep hot until serving. Food poisoning is a nasty and sometimes fatal illness.

Prevent cross contamination. "Cross contamination" is when you "infect" one food product with another. An example of cross contamination is cutting raw chicken and then fruit on the same cutting board without cleaning the board and knife in-between. Handling food without first washing your hands is another no-no. Your hands are petri dishes, too. Main hazards involve handling those perishable, high-protein foods. Handling these foods and then touching other food without washing your hands in-between breeds trouble.

"Bringing to a boil" is a precautionary cooking technique. As water reaches its boiling point of 212°F, this raises the temperature well beyond the danger zone, thereby reducing the risk of food poisoning. Food is then reduced to a simmer, to retain some nutrients.

Cool down. It is important to cool a dish before storing in the refrigerator or freezer. Hot foods may sour if cooled down too quickly, but it may spoil if cooled down too slowly. Cooling needs to be just right.

NOTE: Bringing food to a boil destroys heat-sensitive bacteria, such as *Salmonella*. Some villains—like *E. coli* and *botulism*—are heat-resistant and may survive in boiling liquid.

Remove a cooked dish from its heat source and let it sit on the counter, window, or outside. If cooling a soup, transfer it to another container to hasten its cooling. Poke a few holes in a casserole to release steam. Allow food to sit at least until it is room temperature—about an hour. Cover food well and refrigerate. If planning to freeze food, first chill it overnight in the refrigerator.

Use patience and common sense, follow these precautionary techniques, and food will remain sweet and fresh.

7. RESPECT THE COMFORT ZONE

You've heard this one before: **It is unwise to experiment on company**, when you want to control a meal's successful outcome. This is not to say you cannot be creative; however, be creative in a familiar way. Save imagination and experimentation for times when you are not concerned with making an impression. Enough issues occur with familiar cooking processes—especially if you're a new cook—without adding the extra stress of unknown results. Remember our friend Bridget Jones and her omelet birthday party!

8. COOKING = HEALTH

When you cook for yourself, you control what is going into your body. Cooking for ourselves offer opportunities to FARE WELL, reducing the amount of refined and processed foods we consume. Have your *mise en place*—easy-to-build "prep"—on hand: cooked grains and beans, nut butters, cut vegetables, and dressings. Bake nutritious cookies or breads for immediate meals. Freeze healthy meals for those frenetic days.* The more you cook, the more nutritious food you may have available when in a hurry and need to grab something quickly.

> *I'd rather spend my time cooking than in the doctor's office. I'd rather eat healthy food than medicine.*

Cooking allows more control in our lives. When we cook, we are making conscious choices about what we put into our bodies. When you run out of something, knowing how to cook empowers you. As long as I have oil and vinegar, I will have salad dressing. If I also have an egg, then I will have a supply of mayonnaise.

Stress studies reveal that increasing control over one's life reduces stress responses. Certainly some areas in life are not in our control. But making choices on what foods to prepare for my family is empowering and creates a state of well-being. As the old saying goes, "I'd rather pay the grocer than the doctor." To update this motto, I'd rather spend my time cooking than in the doctor's office. I'd rather eat healthy food than medicine.

*Use frozen food within 2-3 months, as prolonged freezing deteriorates nutrients.

❦   ❦   ❦

Before the carrot incident came the mayonnaise test. It was the first hour on the first day of work at Café du Parc. I'd just washed my hands and put on my chef's coat and apron, then tucked a clean, folded dish rag into my apron. I looked up to see Chef Pierre approaching. A short man, his face gazed up at my nose. Height had no bearing; his stance and manner were intimidating. I focused on his neck and chin, versus confronting him with eyeballing. I tried not to twitch.

"Susanne."
"Yes, Chef."
"Make me a mayonnaise."
"Yes, *Chef!*" Quickly, I lunged into the walk-in to retrieve some eggs and then grabbed the vinegar and vegetable oil from the shelf. The salt and pepper were

already on the counter. With whisk in hand, I began preparing the mayonnaise. I was careful not to add the oil too quickly, as this would upset the emulsion and break the sauce ("Marinades and Dressings" chapter).

When finished, I stood erect, not unlike a private on his first day of boot camp. I would have saluted if asked, I was so nervous.

"Chef, the mayonnaise is ready."

Chef Pierre sauntered over and peered into the bowl. He stuck his nose near the rim and dipped his finger into the bowl. He ran the sauce over his tongue without any change in facial expression. Looking off to the side, contemplating, he took another dip in the sauce. Then a third dip. Finally, after a few minutes (it was probably 10 seconds), he looked at me without grinning and tipped up his chin, indicating an *over there* movement. "Get to work."

He never mentioned it, and I didn't think too much about it, until a few weeks later when another kid arrived. Like me, this guy was from the Culinary Institute of America. I had just graduated; he was still in school, hired as an intern.

Richard showed up in his full *black and whites*, looking like the consummate chef. He possessed a confident air and relaxed gait. Smiling and nodding, he greeted the kitchen staff, acknowledging the dishwasher first (*'sup, dude?*) before addressing Chef Pierre.

"Hey, man. How's it going?"
"Make me a mayonnaise."
"Huh?"
"I say make me a mayonnaise."
"Eh, I don't get what you mean."
"What you mean you don't get what I mean?"
"Well, I don't make mayonnaise."
"You don't make mayonnaise?"
"Well, no. I mean, well . . . *what?"*
"You don't make no mayonnaise?"
"Uh, no, Chef. Who makes mayonnaise?"

Chef Pierre grinned. I pictured a lion licking a mouse. "And, just what happens when you run out of mayonnaise?"

"Well, I dunno. I pick up the phone and, um, you know, order it. And next day, you know. I got a case of mayonnaise."

That was the last sentence Richard spoke. Well, not in his life, but as an intern at Café du Parc. Chef Pierre fired him on the spot.

"Bye-bye, Dick," chef remarked, turning his back on Poor Richard and walking away.

So yes, when you know how to make a mayonnaise, you are empowered in your kitchen, which in turn reduces stress and increases well-being. But I have a confession. That story is not really meant to illustrate empowerment and control. I know that I previously waxed on about how cooks need patience in the kitchen and what a mighty virtue that is, indeed. Surely there is a time for patience and tolerance. Certainly knowing how to cook may improve your health and offer a sense of control in one's culinary environment.

But sometimes, you just got to *86* the dick who doesn't get it.

9. OBSERVE AND RETAIN

Be aware of what goes on in your kitchen. Make mental notes neatly filed away to be recalled. For example: I observe that banana bread takes around 35 minutes to bake. I remember this for the next banana bread I bake. If I decide to make carrot bread next time, I predict that it will bake for around 35 minutes. After it has baked about 20 minutes, I will check the bread every few minutes until it is done.

It's helpful to measure a cup of water or flour and then transfer it into a container—say a yogurt container or an empty glass jar— and see how much "a cup" is in various containers—these containers that I have on hand and can use for measuring when I don't have a measuring cup handy.

Some things to remember in the kitchen include:

- ✔ Measurements

- ✔ Cooking time

- ✔ Combinations of ingredients—good/bad flavor combinations

- ✔ Shelf life of ingredients

- ✔ Preparation time

- ✔ Family's reaction to dishes: *Bings* vs. *Thuds*

- ✔ Fresh produce days at the market

- ✔ Where to shop for organically grown foods—farm stands, markets, and specialty shops

Keep your mind keen and aware. Observe yourself in your kitchen. Make lots of mistakes and learn from them. Soon retaining becomes second nature.

This is a key difference between following a recipe and learning to cook. Following a recipe means reading directions and going through motions. Learning to cook involves understanding the concepts—as with any art or skill. It's the difference between rote memorization and *constructivism* or making meaning. Take learning a language, for example. We can *decode*—learn words, carry a phrase book, and get by without really understanding what others are saying. Or we can *comprehend*—visit the country and immerse ourselves in its culture. And, speaking of comprehending, I offer my favorite tip:

10. COOK FOOD UNTIL IT IS DONE

This sentence seems sarcastic and oversimplified, but it is neither. Everyone wants to know, **"How long do I cook something?" The answer is, "until it is done!!"**

Chef Pierre ran his restaurant in the traditional manner, which included feeding his staff before dinner service. My job included cooking for the "family."

That first night at Café du Parc, after the mayonnaise test, Chef Pierre ordered me to cook the dinner's roast. I asked him for how long to cook it? After glaring at me, he quickly turned away and barked, "Cook it until it's *DONE!*"

Poor Chef Pierre. Here he was, a traditionally trained chef from France. He spent three years washing dishes and another two years rinsing lettuce and *another* year peeling potatoes. It was six years before he could be trusted to touch a knife, and only then, this entailed two years of *turning* carrots (a way of shaping them with a paring knife so they are presented in an appealing oval shape), and still *another* two years prepping salads. After ten years, if you're still in the kitchen, you might be ready to learn how to cook. Perhaps.

You may think French chefs would be 100 years old by the time they learn to cook, but most traditionally trained chefs in France began apprenticing at the tender age of 9 or 10. Now here comes this bozo—a graduate from the Culinary Institute of America, and a *woman*, no less! This *shoemaker* who calls herself a chef after playing for two— TWO—lousy years in an American kitchen has the *nerve* to ask how long to cook a roast! Answering me was a waste of his time.

I only asked him once. After that, I cooked food until it was done.

But Susie . . .

I know, I know. I can hear you now. Again you lament, I don't know how long to cook things! Therefore, the book offers you approximations. These will get you into the ball park, but they won't buy you a beer and a hot dog. The best way—the only way, really—to tell when something is done is to check it. Check on your dish every 5-10 minutes. Observe it. Are the beans hard as a rock? They need more time. Are the vegetables mushy? Have they lost their color? They are overdone. Does the cake still shake in the middle of the pan? It is underdone.

"Cook food until it's DONE!"

10A. CARRY-OVER COOKING

Heated food continues to cook after it is removed from its heat source. For instance, muffins will continue to bake after they are removed from the oven. This is called "carry-over cooking." Similar to underseasoning, we want to err on the side of under-cooking or *just* cooking food, rather than overcooking. Better to have crunchy veggies than mushy ones. You can always cook a little more.

There are basic cooking times; however, some things just take longer (or shorter) to cook sometimes! Altitude, gas vs. electric heat, age and condition of stove, alien life forms landing on your property—these factors affect cooking time. The basic rule is to *sense* the food. You've got five senses, so use them: Smell it. See it. Taste it. Feel its texture in your hands and in your mouth. You will know when that food is done.

And if you don't know, then ask Chef Pierre. He'll be glad to help.

"COOK IT UNTIL IT'S DONE" CHART (IN MINUTES)

FOOD PRODUCT	TIME (approximate)
Pasta	5–10
Vegetables	5–30
Tofu and tempeh	10–15
Grains	20–40
Beans	1–2 hours
Pizza	10–15
Muffins	20–30
Yeasted and quick breads	30 min–1 hour
Pudding	15
Cookies	5–15
Cake	20–30
Pies	30 min–1 hour
Cheesecake	1–2 hours

THE BASIC INGREDIENTS

THE BASIC INGREDIENTS

What's in a Recipe?

The main thing to remember about cooking is that it is not complicated. If you cut vegetables into a bowl and pour oil and vinegar onto them, you have a salad. If you add cooked beans, you have a bean salad. If you add garlic and oregano, you have an Italian bean salad.

Giving fancy names to simple dishes is a culinary game. Actually, there is a joke about it:

> **Q:** What's the difference between Cream of Asparagus soup
> and *Crème d'Asperges?*

> **A:** About five bucks a serving.

Simple foods and procedures given fancy names intimidate us. We put blinders on and let the professional chefs handle those. People treat cooking as they do any trade. When our car needs work, what do we do? We bring it to the shop and pray the mechanic doesn't rob us. It is a frustrating feeling, being an intelligent person without the knowledge to understand what is happening with a particular problem and without the capabilities to tackle the problem ourselves.

So-called "experts" may take advantage of us. We see this all the time with auto mechanics, lawyers, doctors, plumbers, retail businessmen, and yes, with restaurateurs. Create a simple dish, give it a fancy festive label, and charge three times as much as would make an honest profit. Make the name so exotic that the customer would not dare to guess the ingredients, much less attempt to make it. Culinary television shows like *Emeril, No*

Reservations, Iron Chef, and *Hell's Kitchen* have both elevated our awareness and alienated us from our kitchens. Cooking has increasingly become a spectator sport reserved for the pros. It is a source of entertainment kept at arm's length and remote control's distance.

Cooking is easy!
If you can make a mud pie, then you can cook.

The BASIC RECIPE FORMULA is:

1. **NECESSARY (MAIN) INGREDIENTS**
2. **ACCESSORY INGREDIENTS**
3. **SAUCE**

This applies to virtually *any* recipe. Here are some examples, to illustrate:

SALAD:
>Main ingredient: lettuce
>Accessory ingredients: onions, peppers, and tomatoes
>Sauce: oil and vinegar

STEW:
>Main: tofu
>Accessory: carrots, onion, celery, and garlic
>Sauce: gravy

ASIAN NOODLES:
>Main: noodles
>Accessory: broccoli, mushrooms, and bean sprouts
>Sauce: ginger and tamari

TACOS:
>   Main: taco shells and beans
>   Accessory: cabbage, jalapenos, and cilantro
>   Sauce: salsa

FRITTATA:
>   Main: eggs
>   Accessory: broccoli, herbs, and cheese
>   Sauce: milk

ROLL-UPS:
>   Main: tortilla wraps
>   Accessory: mushrooms, spinach, and eggplant
>   Sauce: humus

CHEESE SANDWICH:
>   Main: bread and cheese
>   Accessory: tomato, avocado, and sprouts
>   Sauce: mayonnaise

MUD PIE:
>   Main: mud
>   Accessory: twigs, leaves, and bugs
>   Sauce: pond water

The formula also applies to baking:

MUFFINS:
>   Main: flour, salt, baking powder, baking soda (*dry* ingredients)
>   Accessory: nuts, fruit, flavorings, and spices
>   Sauce: eggs, oil, sweeteners, and milk (*wet* ingredients)

This is a simple, practical way to understand recipes. Take out some cookbooks and see this pattern unfold. You might circle the ingredients and label them "Main," "Accessory," and "Sauce." Recognize this pattern in new recipes. Identify the ingredients when you go out for a meal or look in the deli case. As your understanding increases, your confidence increases. As your confidence increases, the fun increases!

Top Ten Lists

MEALS

MEETZ
   (MEAT SUBSTITUTES)

SEEDS

VEGETABLES

LINKGREDIENTS

CONDIMENTS

HERBS & SPICES

CAVEAT FOR THE TOP TEN LISTS:

The following lists are somewhat arbitrary and subjective. In most magazines, you will find Top Ten lists that contain the healthiest products in the world identified by dedicated researchers who have scoured the planet and unearthed the rarest, most exquisite delicacies with exotic, age-reversing qualities.

These lists aren't those. I choose these grains, beans, seeds, vegetable, herbs, and spices in a jitterbug of compromise: based on their familiarity, accessibility, *and* nutritional value, rather than solely on nutrition. Ingredients should satisfy a range of values. A friend once remarked, "There is the best nutrition, and then there's the best I can do." I wouldn't expect to live solely on superfoods like Acai berries and raw cocoa powder and neither should you.

Again, again, again . . . this is a book on basics. You may add your own favorites or, better yet, create your own Top Ten lists!

As for these ingredients, you'll see common and uncommon foods represented. All of the ingredients are readily found in Natural Foods stores like Whole Foods or Wild Oats, in Natural Foods co-operatives, and increasingly, in mainstream supermarkets.

TOP TEN MEALS

1. BEANS AND RICE

2. STIR-FRY

3. SALAD

4. ROLL-UPS (OR SANDWICHES)

5. CASSEROLE

6. BURGERS

7. SOUPS & STEWS

8. PASTA

9. PIZZA

10. FRITTATA

All of these meals use many of the same ingredients. The differences emerge in their role: main, accessory, or sauce. Basically, we're just Mish Mashing beans, seeds, grains, vegetables and fruits, plus eggs and dairy for extra yumminess.

1. Beans and Rice

Good old beans and rice: This is *the* meal, the sultan of staples, the Bible of basics. Beans and rice can be any combination of grains and beans mixed together or served separately. Serve with any sauce or dressing, accompanied with salad or vegetables. This is the meal that will sustain you. Keep your food simple, and life will follow suit.

2. Stir-Fry

Stir-fry is a meal of vegetables, *meetz,* and nuts or seeds, served over a grain. Stir-frying is a particular cooking technique that combines sautéing and steaming. The result is healthier vegetables, brighter colors, and more vibrant taste.

> TIP: Undercook the veggies a bit— *al dente* or "to the bite," to maximize health and color. Add vegetables in order of cooking time ("Vegetable Rainbow" chapter).

3. Salad

The main ingredients for salads are usually vegetables, with grain and beans as the accessories. But like everything here, that's just a guideline. Salads typically have an acid-based dressing, such as vinegar or lemon juice. Serve salads with a nice side of whole grain bread, grains, or beans.

4. Roll-Ups or Sandwich

A roll-up is any combination of beans, rice, vegetable, *meetz*, and sauce rolled into some wrapper. The wrapper determines the type of roll-up: Pasta sheets make Egg Rolls; wheat tortillas make burritos; corn shells make tacos or tostados; seaweed makes sushi. With bread, we have our quintessential sandwich.

Prepare ingredients in shredded and smaller pieces for roll-ups. Slice or grate vegetables and shred *meetz*. Include beans and grains. Small pieces stick together easier and make a chewier texture. Also, they keep the roll-up neatly assembled. Slice *meetz*, cheeses, and veggies thinly for sandwiches. This creates a more melodious chewing symphony versus clamoring through clunky hunks of food.

I'm a sucker for sandwiches. I'm not talking about slapping together some PB & J and calling it a day. I'm talking about the finest thinly cut servings of *meetz* and cheeses. Then I FARE WELL with the veggies. My sandwiches are works of art, honey.

Here's how to make the ideal sandwich:

✔ Toast the bread slices (for stability).

✔ Place the *meetz* and cheeses on the bottom.

✔ Layer lighter ingredients on top.

✔ If you use avocado or spreads, mash first and then spread them onto the bread, to avoid their smushing out during biting.

✔ Place shredded ingredients such as onions, peppers, or mushrooms next to the *meetz* and cheese to secure them in place.

✔ Cover with full slices of ripe tomato.

✔ Protect the tomato from the top layer of bread with lettuce, which prevents sogginess.

✔ Eat the sandwich promptly, for finest flavor and texture. No

TIP: When assembling sandwiches, practice what good grocers do: Put the heavy items on the bottom shelf.

one likes a soggy sandwich, except maybe for David Sedaris'
father (see *Me Talk Pretty One Day*, 2000).

5. Casserole

From the food dictionary, *casserole:*

> This term refers to both a baking dish and the ingredients it contains.
> Casserole cookery is extremely convenient, because the ingredients are
> cooked and served in the same dish. A 'casserole dish' usually refers to a
> deep, round, ovenproof container with handles and a tight-fitting lid. It can
> be glass, metal, ceramic or any other heatproof material. A casserole's ingre-
> dients can include meat, vegetables, beans, rice and anything else that might
> seem appropriate. Often a topping such as cheese or bread crumbs is added
> for texture and flavor.
> www.epicurious.com/tools/fooddictionary/entry/?id=1738

They prepared it so nicely, so why adjust this literary recipe?

6. Burgers

Take the ingredients you've been using, chop 'em up nice and small—smaller than
in roll-ups or casseroles. Then add a *linkgredient* to create a big blob of stuff. Shape
into patties, fry or bake, and . . . yeehaw . . . Burgers! Burgers are great to cook and
freeze for quick healthy meals. For extra flavor, add cheese to the burger mix. I'm
like Wallace of Wallace and Gromit, when it comes to cheese.

7. Soups and Stews

Soups are a leftover staple. They supply the bridge between leftovers and compost.
Still, please respect the practical soup. It's not merely a weighing station before
86ing food. If you don't believe me, watch episode 116 of *Seinfeld*: "The Soup Nazi."
Just because soup is practical and sustainable doesn't make it bland and boring.

TIP: The main difference
between soups and the other
meals is . . . LIQUID.

Use grains and beans, vegetables, and herbs ("Making Soup from
Scratch"). Season soup according to the international listings ("Top
Ten Herbs & Spices"). Serve soup with vegetable salad and a hearty
chunk of bread with olive oil, butter, or cheese.

8. Pasta

Pasta is basically milled grain and water. Nowadays, pasta is made from most any
grain: wheat, buckwheat, rice, corn, and other gluten-free options, such as soy or
potato. Pasta comes in all kinds of shapes and sizes. Use common sense when

Whole milk is less

processed and offers

more nutrients.

TIP: Undercook the pasta a bit—*al dente*—to maximize texture and flavor.

preparing the accessory ingredients. As with roll-ups, prepare your ingredients to accommodate the pasta shape you choose: Cut thin strips for Angel Hair or Lo Mein and small chunks with spirals.

Check out cool shapes from A-Z, from the National Pasta Association: www.ilovepasta.org/shapes.html or get creative with the Pasta Shoppe: http://pastashoppe.com. (Not your healthiest pasta options, but they sure are fun.)

9. Pizza

Pizza is crust, sauce, cheese, and toppings. Gosh, who doesn't know that, right? Pizza freedom comes in playing with the parts:

CRUST: Shaped pizza dough, pita breads, English muffins, or other flat breads.

SAUCE: Tomato is the default vegetable (technically a fruit, for you food nerds), but thanks to my mom's allergy and creative foodies, there are alternatives to tomato: pesto, creamy cheese, BBQ, guacamole, salsa, or sauce made from vegetables, such as pureed peppers or squash. Beans make an interesting tomato substitute. Experiment with (precooked) red or yellow lentils as the sauce.

CHEESE: Mozzarella, of course, but also try freshly grated parmesans, ricotta, or any cheese that you like. Good-melting cheeses such as Raclette or Gruyere offer a zippy change.

TOPPINGS: What do you like? Put it on your pizza. Heed the layering advice from sandwiches, however; layer heavy ingredients like *meetz* first, and then stack with lighter items like onions and peppers.

The secret to great pizza is to bake it in a HOT OVEN—around 450–500°F—until the pizza bubbles. The edge of the pie lifts easily. The bottom of the crust turns golden brown. Finish pizza with an olive oil drizzle. Do attempt to let piping hot pizza cool down. Pizza right-out-of-the-oven may sound tempting, but it's better to wait. Hot dough tastes gooey, and sizzling sauce burns the roof of your mouth.

10. Frittata

Frittata combines eggs, cheese, and milk. Frittata is a healthier version of quiche—without the crust. It's a lovely way to eat your veggies and *meetz*. Choose fresh whole milk and any cheese. Fry up all the yummy veggies and then pour the frittata mixture over them. Let it slowly cook on top of the stove and, if time, finish cooking in a medium oven.

I recommend WHOLE milk in all cooking. Whole milk is less processed and offers more nutrients. If you are concerned about fat in your diet, then cut out junk food, but retain quality fat from whole nutritious foods—whole milk and cultured milk products, cheeses, whole eggs, olive oil, fish, nuts, and seeds. FARE WELL.

To Meat or Not to Meat?

I didn't intend to create a vegetarian book. I am not a vegetarian. My blood type is O positive, and Os are purported to thrive on animal-based proteins. Heck, I have to agree with this research. I'm more carnivore than omnivore. Once, in college, I went on an all-protein diet—pre-Atkins' hard core. I felt great (except for the part where I didn't have a bowel movement for like three weeks . . .).

When I started working in Health Food stores, I practiced vegetarianism. Intellectually, it just made sense, and so I gave up meat. But somatically, I suffered. I noticed that about every six weeks I would become plagued with intense meat cravings. And it wasn't just meat. I craved the nastiest crop: juicy burgers, spicy pepperonis, greasy sausage. Aaaahhh . . . every six weeks, I'd break down and gobble the beast.

And afterward . . . something would happen. I'd feel better. More awake, alive . . . as if a light had been turned on. This disturbing ritual lasted a few years until I finally acquiesced.

So yes, I eat meat. But to be fair to Mother Earth, one shouldn't. There's just no sound political, physiological, economical, moral, ethical, or financial reason to eat meat anymore. Even when we hunt or raise our own, eating meat on Planet Earth is just a dying game.

But, Susie, if there is no reason to eat meat, why do you still eat it?

Because I'm a hypocrite. I don't know what to tell you. I know I shouldn't eat it, and I know I don't need to. But I like meat, and I feel better when I eat it. What can I say? I do respect the fact that meat production and consumption are wasteful, detrimental acts against our health and our planet. So I cannot with good conscience condone eating meat.

If you do eat meat, remember to FARE WELL. Choose products free of antibiotics, steroids, and mass-production facilities (watch *Food, Inc.*). Whenever possible, choose meat from Natural Foods stores and local farmers. Try your hand at fishing and hunting or buy the meat from those who do. This year, we slaughtered our own broiler chickens—fantastic (almost worth the mass genocide)!

I'm not the patron saint of carnivores. If I'm going out to dinner, I'll eat meat even if I didn't shake the hand of the farmer or pray *Namaste* to the sacrificial fowl who surrendered its life to satisfy my blood type. (*Is it local?* www.ifc.com/videos/portlandia-is-it-local)

When preparing any protein (animal or vegetarian) for your meals, honor the *Deck of Cards* rule: The appropriate protein portion—per meal—is about the size of a deck of cards. U.S. Americans eat way too much protein. Excess protein increases pH acidity through uric acid buildup and can contribute to inflammatory diseases such as arthritis, gout, and indigestion.

There's just no sound political, physiological, economical, moral, ethical, or financial reason to eat meat anymore.

Limit red meat and emphasize fish and poultry. If you are prone to the six-week cravings, include dairy and eggs in your diet. Eating less meat and more quality meat will pay off. Your doctor will thank you for visiting her less. And remember to be gentle with yourself if you do give in to those ferocious pepperonis and sausages. After all, you're only human.

One viable argument remains for eating meat and animal products, including eggs and dairy. Animal products are excellent sources of complete proteins. Complete proteins are protein sources that supply essential amino acids.

Hold up. Complete? Amino acids? Essential??

Right. Sorry. Proteins are made up of amino acids—building blocks or material for basically anything we build and repair in the body: bone, muscle, tissue, fluid, etc. Some amino acids are *nonessential*: We produce these in our body (when we're healthy, that is). Some amino acids must be imported and delivered to us through food. These are *essential*—essential that we consume them. Protein sources that are complete supply all the essential amino acids that humans need. And sure enough, animal-based proteins supply complete proteins. *Rrrowwwf!*

Can you get complete proteins from vegetable sources?

Absolutely. Years ago, hippies used to talk about eating beans and rice together. The reason was that beans had some essential amino acids and rice had others. When eaten together, they'd create a symbiotic amino acid fusion (like, wow)—they'd complement each other and supply all the essential amino acids, thus creating a complete protein. Nowadays, we understand that we don't *literally* need to eat beans and rice *simultaneously* to receive the complete protein. We merely have to include both in our diets.

Do only beans and rice have all the essential amino acids?

Heavens, no. In order to receive all the essential amino acids, simply eat a variety of beans, legumes, nuts, seeds, and grains.

Does any single vegetarian source offer complete protein?

Almonds, quinoa, sesame, and soy products, to name a few. Some seaweed contains complete proteins.

So technically, there is no need to eat meat then . . . is there, Susie?

Ah, shuddap. Stop asking so many questions.

Top Ten Ingredients

TOP TEN MEETZ (meat substitutes)

1. TOFU	6. EGG
2. TEMPEH	7. CHEESE
3. SEITAN	8. EGGPLANT
4. MUSHROOMS	9. OKARA OR QUORN
5. NUTS & SEEDS	10. TVP (TEXTURIZED VEGETABLE PROTEIN)

1. Tofu

Tofu is a staple vegetarian protein made from fermented soybean curd. Tofu is to soybean as cottage cheese is to milk. Tofu comes in different textures: soft, regular, firm, or extra firm. Tofu is basically cooked, although it possesses a neutral flavor. It is intended for marinating and combining. Cut firm tofu in chunks for stir-fry and soups, bake or broil tofu slices as burgers, or crumble into casseroles and roll-ups. Use regular tofu as an egg salad substitute. Use soft tofu in desserts—cheesecake, mousses, whipped cream, and custards. In its natural or "raw" form, it can be used to thicken salad dressings, sauces, and smoothies.

2. Tempeh

Tempeh is also fermented soybean. It differs from tofu in that it uses the whole bean instead of the isolated soy protein. Tempeh's special fermentation process encourages vitamin B12 formation. Tempeh and miso (another soy derivation) provide some of the few vegetarian sources of B12. Tempeh has a very firm texture, making it a great meat substitute. Grate into spaghetti sauce or casseroles for a ground beef flavor and texture. Tempeh must be cooked before eating. Fry it as you would any meat, and serve it in the same ways.

NOTE: Soy allergies are increasing; therefore, observe your body responses after eating tofu and tempeh. If you experience indigestion, you might have a sensitivity to soy.

3. Seitan

Seitan (pronounced *say-tan*) is wheat protein or *gluten*. Wheat flour and water make dough, which is then soaked completely to remove the grain's starch. What's left is primarily wheat gluten. The result is a chewy, spongy, meatloaf-like product. Use seitan as you would tempeh or firm tofu.

4. Mushrooms

Mushrooms offer rich, fulfilling flavor and texture to foods and sauces. Mushrooms are high in protein and fiber. Grind mushrooms with onion, garlic, and spices to create vegetarian *pate*. (This is actually a product called *duxelle*—used in Beef Wellington.) Include mushrooms in any meal to increase the protein content of your dish.

5. Nuts & Seeds

Since nuts are high in protein, they make fine meat alternatives. Plus they offer better-burning fuel in the form of unsaturated (vegetable) fats, compared with the harder-to-burn saturated (animal) fats. Use nut butters in sauces, spread on breads, fruit and vegetables, and toss in salads. Sauté whole nuts whole and include in soups and stir-fry dishes.

6. Egg

Eggs give body and sustenance to dressings, salads, and casseroles. They are used in desserts to create a smooth and creamy texture. Egg protein is complete and mimics the protein requirements of humans in amino acid profiles. As eggs are an animal product, however, please use moderately. Purchase eggs from local farms; you will taste the difference.

TIP: Try duck eggs! They are bigger, creamier, and healthier.

7. Cheese

Cheese, like egg, is a complete protein, but it is also generally higher in harder-to-burn saturated fat than vegetable protein. Cheese is a satisfying substitute if you are cutting down on meat. It is indispensable for flavor in meals, especially casseroles, frittatas, or Mexican foods. I love a simple meal of good cheese with home-baked bread. Use cheese as a condiment rather than the meal's staple, and enjoy it for the rich treat that it is.

8. Eggplant

Eggplant has a meaty texture and taste—more so than other vegetables. Because of this, it plays the meat role in *Ratatouille*, Eggplant Parmesan, and stir-fry. Eggplant is the main ingredient in *Baba Ganoush* (delightful garlicky spread). Add it to stir-fry, roll-ups, pizzas, and salads to make a light meal more satisfying.

9. Okara Or Quorn

Okara is the high-fiber by-product of soybean, when making tofu. Okara's texture is quite firm and makes a great chicken substitute. *Quorn* is a mushroom-based protein gaining popularity. Both are typically sold pre-seasoned as patties or nuggets. Find them in the freezer section of Natural Foods markets.

10. TVP

TVP, or Texturized Vegetable Protein, is used as a substitute for ground meat. TVP is pre-cooked, dried soy protein. First rehydrate and then cook it:

→ Boil 2 parts liquid for 1 part TVP

→ Pour boiling liquid over TVP

→ Cover and let sit for 5–10 minutes.

→ Add to chili, casseroles, or blend into loaf dishes.

→ For extra flavor, fry it before adding to meals.

TOP TEN SEEDS

1. RICE	6. ALMOND
2. ADUKI	7. MILLET
3. SESAME	8. BARLEY
4. LENTIL	9. PUMPKIN
5. CHICK PEA / GARBANZO BEAN	10. WHEAT

Beans, grains, legumes, peas, seeds . . . these are often logged as separate categories, but they are all plant seeds. Seeds are also used for sprouting ("Wild Things" chapter).

1. Rice

Starting with the staples, let's begin with rice—whole grain brown rice, that is. Rice grows in long, medium, and short grains. There are dozens of varieties, including the lighter, whiter Basmati or the provocative grass seed, wild rice. Rice offers fiber, B vitamins, minerals, and Essential Fatty Acids (EFAs), which are needed for brain function, energy, and hormonal regulation.

2. Aduki

2. Aduki (also *Azuki,* or *Adzuki*) beans are hailed as one of the healthiest of all the beans. These little red babies earn gold stars in nutrition and flavor. All beans earn nutritional stars in cooking, and popular ones include Black Turtle, Kidney, and Black-Eyed Peas. But in terms of nutrient density, Aduki comes out on top. In the East, Aduki beans are known as the "Mercedes" of beans. They are also one of the smallest beans, so crazybusy lifestyles appreciate their speedy cooking time (about 1 hour). Aduki beans are low-fat and high-protein. They possess a natural sugar profile, making them one of the few beans that one might use in desserts and baking.

3. Sesame

Sesame seeds are nutritious and versatile: whole as seed, pureed as *tahini,* or toasted and pressed as oil. Sesame seeds score high in supplying EFAs. Sesame seeds offer high sources of trace minerals and complete protein. Open, sesame!

4. Lentil

Lentils earn top honors: low in saturated fat, cholesterol, and sodium and high in protein, iron, phosphorus, and copper. They are an excellent source of dietary fiber, Folic acid, and manganese. Lentils are delicious, but consume with a word of warning: They do create quite a stir . . . in the nether regions, if you know what I mean.

5. Chick Pea / Garbanzo Bean

Used whole in meals or pureed in humus, chick peas are a popular choice of legume. Chick peas also are ground fine and used for tortillas, binding burgers, or as a gluten-free flour substitute in breads and pizza dough. Chick peas are rich in minerals, including copper, iron, and magnesium, and provide a healthy dose of Folic acid—the B vitamin associated with prenatal health.

6. Almond

Almonds are one of the few vegetarian sources of complete protein; they are loaded with the stuff. Almonds are rich suppliers of minerals. For those avoiding dairy products, almonds are nature's calcium supplement. Plus they are adaptable: whole in meals, pureed as almond butter in sandwiches and sauces, or enjoyed whole—raw or toasted—as a healthy snack. My favorite mini-meal is tamari-roasted almonds. I'm eating them right now, as I edit this book.

7. Millet

Millet has a sweet nutty flavor, tender bumpy texture, and pretty yellow color. It's a friendly grain and a pleasant substitute for the usual rice. Millet makes my list, as it contains rich amounts of the elusive vitamin B17 (laetrile) and the lesser-known B15 (pangamic acid). These B vitamins are used in alternative cancer treatments in other (non-U.S.) countries.

In the United States, the medicinal form of laetrile is illegal, thanks to the stupidity of a few people who follow the credo: *Anything worth doing is worth overdoing.* One couple, hearing about the powerful anticancer properties of laetrile, consumed excessive amounts of this vitamin and died. Like most potent medicines, a little laetrile goes a long way. And the best way to consume vitamin B17—or any vitamin for that matter—is through your food sources, rather than in isolated form.

I eat four apricot kernels a day, and I am not dead.

What other food sources contain laetrile?

Laetrile is commonly found in many fruits, leafy greens, beans, and nuts. The seeds of fruit contain especially high amounts. One potent source is apricot kernels. These are not sold in the United States but may be purchased online. www.apricotpower.com

8. Barley

Barley's an unsung hero, a true workhorse of grains. Barley wows soups, salads, and casseroles. Its chewy texture is great in bread. Barley flakes are super yummy as breakfast cereal or in cookies, and the flour works well as a wheat substitute. My favorite gingerbread uses barley flour. Barley is high in protein and EFAs and is a rich source of manganese and selenium—minerals linked to healthy immune systems.

9. Pumpkin

Pumpkin seeds are yummy—buttery, sweet, and addictive. Toasted or raw pumpkin seeds are a healthier alternative to peanuts and less expensive than almonds. Add them whole to salads, casseroles, and burgers. Ground pumpkin seeds thicken sauces and create a unique special flavor. Pumpkin seeds are a rich source of EFAs, but their claim to fame is their levels of zinc. Zinc is the "traffic cop," facilitating absorption and utilization of a variety of nutrients, proteins, and enzymes. It also has the reputation for being the "male mineral"—promoting healthy male sexual function and performance.

10. Wheat

I list wheat last, out of respect for our changing cultural climate. As wheat allergies and insensitivities continue to rise (bad pun intended), people seek wheat-free alternatives. Avoiding wheat and peanuts is now as popular as PB & J sandwiches used to be.

That being said, wheat is still the primary grain for pastas, breads, and cereals. When choosing wheat, go for organic whole grain wheat or wheat's "cousin" grains, spelt and einkorn. And to be fair to wheat, it is a nutritional powerhouse, supplying vitamins (especially Bs), EFAs, minerals, protein, and fiber.

TOP TEN VEGETABLES

1. ONION	6. POTATO
2. CARROT	7. PEPPER
3. CELERY	8. BROCCOLI
4. LEAFY GREENS	9. CORN
5. TOMATO	10. OLIVE

Vitamin B12 is rarely found in vegetarian diets. Interestingly, one unlikely source is in the *dirt* that is found on the skins of plants. Clean your veggies, but don't feel the need to scrub them like your toilet; just rinse them well. Leave the peel on more tender veggies like potatoes and carrots. I leave the skin on beets, turnips, and rutabagas and then peel after cooking. Cooking with the skins on adds nutrients to the liquid. Reuse the liquid for soups and sauces.

1, 2, & 3. Onion, Carrot, & Celery

This trio is at the foundation of many Top Ten Meals, especially soups, burgers, casseroles, and stir-fry. They form the famed *Brunoises Triumvirate* (three things chopped up really finely) in French cuisine. Small dices of these dudes supply the basis for many recipes. They are so common that you may not even realize it. Pick up any book on French cuisine and you'll find them. Or *Forget Paris*; scan soup labels or frozen burger packages—just about any packaged food—and you'll discover this omnipotent trio.

4. Leafy Greens

Leafy greens are the nutritional superstars, winning races in vitamins A, B, C, E, and K, trace and major minerals, enzymes, and proteins. They are high in fiber and low in calories. Kale, spinach, and chard are among the most common, but do expand your horizons: Bok choy, tatsoi, or dark beauties like dandelion and nettle. Try tangy herbs like arugula and watercress, and remember to FARE WELL.

5. Tomato

Tomato is the MVP of vegetables in terms of versatility. Tomatoes score straight A's in durability and adaptability. Tomatoes are the backbone in soups, salads, sauces, and—you know what? They are everywhere.

☛ A caution with tomatoes is that they are a member of the nightshade family. Nightshade plants have been linked to arthritis due to antagonistic reactions from the plant's chemicals called *alkaloids*. If you are arthritic, you might try to reduce your consumption of this vegetable family, which includes tomato, potato, eggplant, and peppers.

6. Potato

Potatoes are as common and versatile as tomatoes. I'm sorry, but they are too darned good to leave off the list. I keep the skin on when cooking, but I have read that the potato may be more nutritious without the skin. My stubborn mind can't wrap its head around that "logic," so I leave the skins on, even in mashed potatoes.

Like tomatoes, potatoes are a member of the nightshade family, so approach their use as you might for any nightshade vegetable. Choose organic local potatoes. Commercially-grown potatoes receive an especially bad rap these days, as they are grown with more pesticides and herbicides than most other produce.

7. Peppers

So many peppers, so little time . . . I love my food hot, so peppers make my Top Ten list. Red peppers contain more vitamin C than oranges, and only strawberry leaves (yes, the *leaves*) beat peppers for the C-trophy. Peppers are heavy hitters in most Top Ten meals and again . . . the *hots* . . . dozens of varieties of peppers in varying degrees of heat ignite the sass in your kitchen. Cayenne contains *capsicum*, which offers pain-relieving qualities and has been used to treat ulcers and digestive disorders. That pain heals. Bring on the heat!

8. Broccoli

Before sexy leafy greens hit the Foodie scene, good ol' broccoli and its brassica pals were the Big Boys of the nutritional vegetable kingdom. Broccoli is touted as the anticancer veggie. Like all green veggies, it is high in water-soluble vitamins B complex and C, beta-carotene, antioxidants, minerals, and immune-building proteins. Growing up, *Broccoli au Gratin* was my favorite vegetable dish.

9. Corn

Corn is one of the most popular plants in America; it's so popular that our government pays farmers to grow it. Corn creates hundreds of products and by-products: high fructose corn syrup, ethanol, aspirin, batteries, paper plates, explosives, and asbestos. So naturally, I now consider corn to be the Devil and hate to promote it.

But, shucks. I rely on corn for my tortillas and wouldn't let a summer go by without freshly steamed Silver Queen ears from the garden. One of my favorite foods is tamales, and corn is the main ingredient. When buying corn, as with any food product, FARE WELL: Buy locally grown corn and whole corn tortillas free of hydrogenated oil. My favorite brand is Maria & Ricardo's. They fry up soft and chewy. www.mariaandricardos.com

And try not to obsess about King Corn taking over the planet!

10. Olives

Olives contain olive oil, which is one of the healthiest oils. Olives span many ethnicities, enhancing European, Mediterranean, and Middle Eastern cuisines. They enliven a soup or salad and taste great with roll-ups. Olives are brutes; they stand alone with bread and cheese. And after all, a martini ain't a martini without one. Avoid canned black olives; they offer the least nutrition and flavor. Olives are readily available in bulk salad bars, stuffed with exotic garnishes, and ready to party.

TOP TEN *LINKGREDIENTS*

1. FLOUR	6. YOGURT
2. BREAD CRUMBS	7. POTATO
3. KUZU	8. BROWN RICE
4. MAYONNAISE	9. AVOCADO
5. TAHINI	10. BLENDER

*Linkgredient*s are used for linking soups, sauces, burgers, and casseroles. They are the thickeners, combiners, emulsifiers, extenders, and blenders of the culinary world.

1. (Whole Wheat) Flour

A staple thickener of soups and sauces, flour is the most common and least expensive option. Always have flour available for last minute linking. White flour is smoother, but whole wheat offers more nutrients.

2. Bread Crumbs

Bread crumbs are a practical, economical form of conservation. Save loaf ends and old bread for crumbing. Bread crumbs are handy when a casserole or dessert is too wet and you need to improvise. They swiftly turn leftover casseroles into yummy burgers.

3. Kuzu

Macrobiotic and Traditional Chinese Medicine (TCM) hail kuzu as a digestive wonder, aiding in restoring bacterial flora and alleviating stomach and intestinal disorders. Kuzu is sold in Natural and Asian Foods stores and is beginning to find its way into mainstream markets. Because of its health benefits, kuzu is preferable to arrowroot or cornstarch. To use kuzu, melt a chunk in cold water, creating a milk-like consistency. Then add to boiling soups or sauce. You can also add powdered kuzu to thicken burger and casserole mixtures.

4. Mayonnaise

Mayonnaise marries ingredients, soothes texture, and tickles flavor. It provides a sweet undercurrent to many dishes. Combining with water creates instant creamy dressing. Mayonnaise is the salad maker: Chopped veggies become cole slaw, diced tofu becomes mock egg salad, and pasta becomes . . . well, pasta salad. What sandwich would be linked without mayo? I admit that I'm biased. I adore mayonnaise; it's the Captain to my Tennille.

My favorite mayonnaise comes from the folks at *Follow Your Heart:* www.followyourheart.com/products/grapeseed-vegenaise/.

This mayo is made from grapeseed oil, which rivals olive oil in health benefits. Grapeseed oil is one of the few natural foods known to raise HDL, aka the "good" cholesterol. It is mountain-high in EFAs and antioxidants. Grapeseed has a high burning temperature too, so it is a great choice for frying without destroying the oil's nutrients (olive oil has a low burning temperature).

5. Tahini or Sesame Butter

Tahini is paste from hulled or unhulled sesame seeds. Tahini is sticky and links ingredients well in casseroles, pastas, and stir-fry. Substitute tahini for egg or dairy in sauces and dressings. It lends a wonderful buttery nutty flavor in desserts. Tahini is available raw and roasted. Try both; their flavors are quite different.

6. Yogurt

Although dairy allergies are common, many people can tolerate yogurt. Used as a condiment, yogurt is valuable in cooking. It is a creamy, tangy addition. When possible, add yogurt to your food *after* cooking, to preserve its friendly bacterial cultures.

7. Egg

Egg, like yogurt, is the hidden ingredient that emulsifies many dishes. "Emulsify" is the fancy term for making creamy. Technically, the egg protein binds oil to acid, usually vinegar. Emulsion is the arbitration between these two opposing forces.

Egg's potential exceeds creamy dressings. Eggs are the base of frittatas. They bind burgers and casseroles. Eggs also improve texture and help baked goods to rise. Substitute tofu for egg if you prefer a vegetarian option. And remember to try those duck eggs. Quack.

8. Potato

Potato thickens soup. Add small dices or shredded potato; they dissolve into the liquid and make it creamy. If you want a broth or noncreamy soup base, add bigger chunks. Shredded potatoes thicken casseroles and burgers. Add leftover potatoes into frittatas. Cold diced potatoes make awesome salads—with mayonnaise, of course.

9. Brown Rice

Like potato, brown rice thickens and binds many dishes. Add uncooked brown rice into a soup; it will thicken and add sustenance as it simmers. Use cooked rice in casseroles and veggie burgers to bind ingredients. Add it to breads, cookies, and puddings for a chewy texture.

10. Avocado

Avocado is delightfully useful for thickening salad dressings and sauces. It provides a healthier substitute for mayonnaise. Combine avocado with mustard or herbs for a zippy sandwich spread. Avocado can also be used to thicken cold soups. Although it is a fruit, use avocado moderately, as it is does contain saturated fat.

. . . And the number one way to thicken? The Hand-held Immersion Blender!

Blending is the ideal thickener. It thickens with no added fat, sugar, salt, or calories! Shake oil, vinegar, and egg; you have a vinaigrette. Blend this vinaigrette and you have creamy mayonnaise. A blender thickens soups, sauces, and dressings. It can smooth a lumpy pudding. Blenders are indispensable for shakes and chilly exotic drinks. What's better than the blender? Hand-held or immersion blenders! They are awesome: lightweight, portable, easy to clean, and affordable. I use this little dynamo about every day. Retire that old clunky blender and get yourself a hand-held—I'm telling you!

TOP TEN CONDIMENTS

1. SALT & PEPPER	6. TAHINI
2. TAMARI	7. MISO
3. SWEETENER	8. BRAGG'S LIQUID AMINOS
4. OLIVE OIL	9. SPIKE
5. VINEGAR	10. BRONNER'S BALANCED MINERAL SEASONING

1. Salt & Pepper

Keep it salty, sweetheart. FARE WELL foods are so tasty that all you really need to season them with is a touch of salt and pepper. I use a hand mill for both salt and pepper and grind 'em, fresh. Whether or not you grind, use whole sea salt instead of iodized "table salt." Table salt contains only isolated sodium chloride, whereas whole sea salt supplies a broad spectrum of necessary, balanced minerals—sodium, potassium, magnesium, and calcium—to name a few. Table salt also (unnecessarily) adds iodine, sugar, and anticlogging agents. Again, it's all about nutrient density; make your food choices count.

2. Tamari

Tamari is the quintessential seasoning; use it on anything (excluding desserts) to develop food's natural flavors. Tamari is a sauce made from fermented soybeans and wheat. Think of it as soy sauce without added table salt, sugar, or MSG. *Shoyu* is a lighter, less pungent tamari. Both are available in wheat-free and low-sodium options.

3. Sweetener

Sometimes you will try to duplicate a recipe and cannot match the flavor. There is a missing taste—a certain "something." Often that something is sweetener. Sweetener mellows the flavor of a dish and softens its edges.

TIP: Choose whole or complex sugars such as rice syrup, maple syrup, or agave rather than simple white sugar. These natural sugars have more complex carbohydrates.

4. Olive Oil

Considered the most nutritious, olive oil is high in monounsaturated fat. It contains *squalene*—a powerful antioxidant, highly beneficial to the immune system. Olive oil offers a rare vegetarian source of squalene (most commonly found in shark's liver). Olive oil also supplies vitamins A, K, and E. Olive oil's pungency is inappropriate for some recipes (especially dessert), so substitute with other oils for a more delicate flavor. For a neutral substitute, grapeseed oil is a great choice.

In general, choose unrefined, organic oils. Their tastes and smells are more pungent due to healthier processing, which retains more nutrients. Store healthy oils in cool dark places, as heat and light can destroy their nutrients.

☛ AVOID HYDROGENATED OR TRANS-FAT OILS

Hydrogenated or trans-fat oils are vegetable oils that, through chemical manipulation, maintain a solid state at room temperature. Hydrogenated oils break down inefficiently in the body. If overly consumed, these trans-fats may block blood vessels or intestinal walls and contribute to stroke, heart attack, and colonic diseases.

> TIP: If your mental model insists upon something solid and creamy to spread upon your bread at room temperature, use butter.

5. Vinegar

Vinegar adds tang, balances the oil in recipes, and complements many foods. Vinegar is acidic and is used to marinate and tenderize. Vinegar and oil alone could provide the sauce for most vegetables, or any dish, for that matter.

Use raw, nonpasteurized, and undistilled vinegar. Distilled and pasteurized vinegars hinder digestion, while raw vinegar offers a wealth of health benefits, especially as a digestive tonic. Choose Raw Apple Cider Vinegar or Raw Red Grape (alternative to wine vinegar). Popular brands are *Bragg's* and *Eden Foods*.

6. Tahini

Tahini is available raw and toasted. It is a valuable condiment that makes things go creamy. Use it in sauces, dressings, and sandwich spreads. Tahini supplies a complete protein for the human body and is high in minerals, especially calcium.

THE VEGETARIAN CHEF

7. Miso

Miso is fermented soybean paste. Use miso as you would bouillon or soup base. It possesses a sweet, salty flavor. It provides an abundant source of complete protein, live enzymes, and calcium. The fermentation process initiates vitamin B12 production, making miso an elusive vegetarian source of this typically animal-derived vitamin.

Miso is known for its blood-purifying properties. Anecdotes regale it as such a valuable blood cleanser that Japanese police officers who direct traffic drink miso soup every day for lunch to prevent toxic car fumes from accumulating in their bodies. Fermented foods supply healthy bacteria, which comforts the digestive system. Miso is high in minerals that support elimination and enhance the immune system. So, you know . . . miso's really good for you. Lotta nutritional bang for your buck.

Miso is traditionally made from soybeans, although now there are many varieties. In fact, miso is produced from almost any grain or bean. **Hey lady! There are *over 30 varieties* of miso for that Cream of Cauliflower soup!** (I'm sorry, I couldn't resist. Do you think she's reading this?)

8. Bragg's Liquid Aminos

Bragg's Liquid Aminos is a gluten-free, low-sodium substitute for tamari or soy sauce. It provides a rich source of both essential and nonessential amino acids, making it a vegetarian option for complete protein.

9. Spike

Spike is a combination of 39 herbs and spices. It has a delightfully unique flavor. The main ingredient is nutritional yeast, which you will read about next..

10. Nutritional Yeast

Long heralded as an "energy food," nutritional yeast is high in protein, iron, B vitamins, and zinc. It possesses a cheesy nutty flavor that tastes great in salads, dressings, soups, and on sandwiches and popcorn.

My favorite sauce for grains is the Super-Healthy-Yummy-Dressing ("Marinades and Dressings" chapter). The yummy Rice-a-Roni flavor has both children and junk food junkies gobbling it up!

Okay, I lied. I have two more nutrient-dense condiments that warrant props:

11. Jenson's Vegetable Seasoning

Jensen's makes an exquisite seasoning from dried raw vegetable powders. This seasoning can stand alone like salt and pepper, but with more nutrient density. Try it first before further seasoning.

12. Dr. Bronner's Balanced Mineral Seasoning

This salty seasoning can be your best source for trace minerals. It's liquid gold, nutrition-wise. Use it with other seasonings as its flavor may be too "oceany"—sweet, salty, and fishy—by itself. Since his death, Dr. Bronner's food items are now difficult to find. They may, in fact, be discontinued. So if you see this seasoning on shelves, nab it! It may be gone the next time you go shopping.

TOP TEN HERBS & SPICES

1. SALT & PEPPER	6. CUMIN
2. GARLIC	7. THYME
3. PARSLEY	8. CURRY
4. CILANTRO	9. GINGER
5. BASIL	10. PAPRIKA

1. Salt & Pepper

First and foremost, salt and pepper are the Adam and Eve of spices. They are used in just about every dish. Choose whole sea salt. Grind your salt and pepper from hand mills; the taste is more fresh and vibrant.

2. Garlic

Garlic is represented all over the world. I bet when we colonize on Mars, space emigrants will pack garlic. Garlic~ sigh~ that's it. What can I say? That is all you need. Garlic is my favorite spice. I'd put it in pancakes slathered with mayonnaise syrup, if my family would let me get away with it.

Garlic is as medicinal as it is delicious. It has as many many—oh so many—health-promoting benefits as uses in the kitchen. Garlic's properties are beneficial to heart health, including circulatory concerns, high cholesterol, hypertension, and diabetes. Garlic possesses antibiotic, antifungal, and antimicrobial properties. It is one of the few natural (and readily available) antiviral herbs. If you have just one herb in your kitchen, whether on Earth or Mars, let it be garlic.

Food nerds may challenge garlic as an herb or a spice. About.com has this to say on the matter:

> One of the most important ingredients in all of the culinary arts, garlic nevertheless seems to defy, or transcend, attempts to define it in any but the most literal of terms. So, what *is* garlic? Is it an herb? A spice? The truth is, it's neither. The word herb denotes something green, whether the leaves or stems of some sort of plant. The word spice indicates any other item, including roots, bark, seeds and so on, but specifically in the dried form. Garlic really doesn't fit either one of those categories. So it's

probably most accurate to call garlic a vegetable, even though it's hardly ever eaten on its own. In this sense garlic is most similar to onions and shallots, although ultimately garlic belongs in a category all its own."

Here's the thing. When you buy garlic in supermarkets, you're just purchasing the bulb. But when you grow it or shop at local farm stands, you'll have access to the sweet green shoots, or *scapes,* and the tender leaves. And, in this way, garlic is an herb. Nyaah.

3. Parsley

"The finer the parsley, the finer the restaurant." That's what great chefs say when referring to their chopped parsley. Back in culinary school, we chopped parsley until it was a liquid paste. Then we'd wrap it in a dish rag and rinse the parsley, removing that pesky green juice (the healthiest part, brimming with nutrient-rich chlorophyll). When it was clean and dry and beaten into submission, we'd serve it.

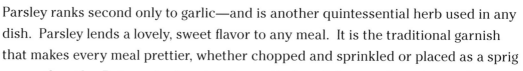

Parsley ranks second only to garlic—and is another quintessential herb used in any dish. Parsley lends a lovely, sweet flavor to any meal. It is the traditional garnish that makes every meal prettier, whether chopped and sprinkled or placed as a sprig on the side. But parsley is not just a pretty face; it is a nutritional powerhouse. Parsley is rich in chlorophyll—a potent blood purifier. Parsley root tea is used as a liver detoxifier. Parsley grows easily in gardens. It is vigorous and renewable; cut the leaves, and it grows right back. It grows well in both cool and warm climates. You can use the whole plant, too. Parsley root is a lesser known vegetable but offers a *root-ish* flavor, like parsnip or celeriac.

4. Cilantro

Cilantro complements foods from Mexico to Malaysia. It's referred to as "Chinese parsley" and is equally nutritious and delicious.

Here's the weird thing about cilantro. There are two distinct cilantro camps: Love and Hate. There ain't no middle ground. Physiologically, it's purported that there are taste receptors on the buds that actually respond to cilantro's unique flavor. So people are either attracted to or repelled by its flavor. Personally, I'm a lover. I could bathe in the stuff while I scrub my skin with garlic pancakes and marinate my hair with mayonnaise. Eating cheese sandwiches.

5. Basil

Basil's tangy hearty flavor punches any meal. It grows in many varieties, from sweet lemon to dark purple. Basil is awesome in soups, salads, and sauces. Its juice aids digestion and prevents colic or gas.

6. Cumin

Cumin seasons with delicious pungency. It provides richness in the flavor that develops over time. Cumin is fundamental in Mexican, Indian, and Mediterranean cookery. Cumin, like basil, assists in positive digestion.

7. Thyme

Thyme's piquant flavor adds boldness to soups, stews, casseroles, and sauces. In herbal remedies, thyme is used as an expectorant and demulcent, aiding in the relief of coughs, colds, and flus. Thyme is a perennial that grows vigorously in most gardens and comes in many varieties.

8. Curry

Curry is a combination of over a dozen spices that create a unique Middle Eastern flavor and color to foods. Like most herbs and spices, curry possesses health-promoting qualities. Curry aids digestion and elimination. It contains turmeric, which contains the bioflavonoid *quercetin*—an anti-inflammatory agent. Curry is helpful with inflammatory ailments such as arthritis and gout.

9. Ginger

Add ginger to stir-fry, sauces, and marinades . . . drink ginger tea . . . enjoy gingerbread and molasses cookies . . . nibble on crystalized ginger after a meal. Ginger possesses a sweet hot flavor that punches and tickles any tongue it touches. Ginger tea has long been associated as a remedy for nausea, colic, indigestion, low blood pressure (bringing heat to the body), and motion sickness. Crystalized ginger promotes digestion after a heavy or late meal.

10. Paprika

The word *paprika* means *pepper*. Paprika is actually a spice made from dried ground peppers. Paprika is prevalent in Europe, Asia, and the Middle East. It adds heat, robust flavor and color, boosting and rounding out soups and sauces. Paprika creates a richness and astoundingly beautiful color. But be warned: Paprika comes in a range of heats as well. Peppers supply natural pain-relieving compositions and can aid in inflammatory problems, like ulcers and arthritis.

INTERNATIONAL FLAVORS

ITALIAN	MEXICAN	INDIAN
Basil	Chili powder	Curry
Oregano	Cumin	Ginger
Bay Leaf	Cilantro	Basil
Marjoram	Cayenne	Mint
Parsley	Paprika	Anise
Thyme	Tomato	Yogurt
Fennel	Onion	Tomato
Tomato	Lime	Saffron
Porcini Mushrooms	Cinnamon	Turmeric

ORIENTAL	MEDITERRANEAN	FRENCH
Tamari	Olive oil	Wine
Ginger	Lemon	Parsley
Rice vinegar	Oregano	Shallots
Sesame oil	Parsley	Cream
Mirin	Olives	Softened butter
Hot pepper oil	Fennel	Sorrel
Mustard	Cumin	Chervil
Wasabi	Yogurt	Savory
"5- Spice" seasoning	Feta cheese	Nutmeg
Hoison sauce	Honey	Dill

FLAVOR COMBINATIONS

TANGY	SWEET	PUNGENT	SPICY
Basil	Allspice	Black pepper	Cayenne
Chives	Anise	Cumin	White pepper
Dill	Cardamom	Thyme	Garlic
Marjoram	Cinnamon	Bay leaf	Chili powder
Parsley	Cloves	Celery seed	Paprika
Cilantro	Coriander	Curry	Hot peppers
Sage	Fennel	Caraway	
Sorrel	Mace	Rosemary	
Savory	Nutmeg	Oregano	
Anise	Ginger	Tarragon	
Mustard	Mint	Turmeric	
		Lemongrass	
		Chocolate	

Garlic, salt, and pepper are included in every listing.

Seasoned with Accomplishment

Story from the original No Recipe Cookbook version, *circa 1990:*

I learned a valuable lesson from my son today. Sammy is one year old, and bless his heart, he wants to do everything himself and his way. Today we were eating squash, or rather, I was eating squash and feeding him small bits from my finger. After two or three "bits," he wanted no part of my finger and pushed it away. Next I lay the bowl down, thinking he wanted to play with the food.

He did not want the bowl. I picked up the bowl and began eating again. He started whining loudly and kept reaching for the bowl. *What does he want?* I wondered. Intuition replied, *Give him the spoon.*

I handed him the spoon. He immediately stopped whining and began to feed himself. He took some bites, looked at me, smiled, and then held the spoon out to feed me. I ate the squash happily. We began a rhythm: I put squash into the spoon. He would eat some and then feed me. I noticed how much I was enjoying the squash. "Seasoned with accomplishment," I mused, "food tastes sweeter."

Author's note: Sam turned twenty-three this year. He still wants to feed himself. I still want to do it for him. Bless my heart.

THE BASIC
PROCEDURES

THE BASIC PROCEDURES

Three Basic Steps

There are three basic recipe steps in cooking:

> **1. PREPARE THE INGREDIENTS**
>
> **2. COMBINE THE INGREDIENTS**
>
> **3. ADJUST THE INGREDIENTS**

Prepare the ingredients has two substeps: *Prepare the ingredients* and *prepare the utensils.*

1A. PREPARE THE INGREDIENTS

Now that you are cooking with *mise en place*, you know the ingredients before you begin. Bring out all the ingredients at once, prepare them, and put them aside or in the refrigerator to use as needed. This avoids congested countertops (Virtue # 6: Cleanliness).

A few tips, plus the book sections that cover these:

- ✔ If you are preparing protein items, (Top Ten *Meetz*) keep them refrigerated while preparing grains and vegetables (Tip # 6: Cook safely).

- ✔ Marinating any items first (or the day before) allows ample time to develop flavor and texture.

- ✔ Keep marinated food in the refrigerator until cooking ("Marinades and Dressings").

1B. PREPARE THE UTENSILS

Preparing the utensils is crucial. Suppose I'm preparing five gallons of chili. I have my ingredients cut and ready to be cooked. I reach into the cupboard to grab a pot.

D'OH!

I discover that there is no pot big enough to cook all that chili. Now I'll have to cook it in smaller batches. This alters my preparation, performance, and cooking time. And it certainly affects when I'm serving my five gallons of chili to dozens of Super Bowl fans. Instead of a half-time feast, I'm offering them doggie bags to take home. That's a not-so-super bowl of chili, dude.

Basic list of utensils:

- POTS: stainless steel, glass, or cast iron

- PANS: stainless steel, copper, glass, cast iron

- BOWLS: large and small, stainless steel, glass, wooden, ceramic (avoid plastic, when possible)

- COLANDERS: large and small, stainless steel

- STRAINERS: large and small

- SPOONS: solid and slotted, wooden or stainless steel

- SPATULAS: pan, baking, bowl scrapers

- LADLES: large and small, stainless steel

- GRATER: a solid one will save your knuckles

- VEGETABLE PEELER

- TURNING FORK TONGS

- WHISK

- HAND-HELD (IMMERSION) BLENDER

- FUNNELS: large and small

- KNIFE SHARPENER, OR *STEEL*

- SHARPENING STONE

And the most important utensil of all?

- KNIVES! Really really *really* good knives! French or Japanese, please.

☞ **KEEP KNIVES SHARP!**
Dull knives are more dangerous than sharp ones, because they slip.

While it's nice to have a variety of knives, all you really need are three:

1. **CHEF'S:** or *French* or *utility* knife (general use)

2. **SERRATED:** slicing breads and soft items (tomatoes or tofu)

3. **PARING:** for small or fine cuts

These will serve you well. Visit a culinary shop and ask them for a good German brand like *Henkel*. Happily drop a C-note on your knives. They last a lifetime, and you will be grateful for every clean slice. My knives have lasted longer than most of my friendships and all of my marriages, combined. I still have my original French knife from the early 80s. It's a tank. Some chefs prefer Japanese knives, which stay wonderfully sharp. I kick it old school with my European babes.

It is essential to keep knives sharp. Ask your friendly hardware clerk about sharpening knives with a *steel*. If you are serious about cooking, ask for assistance with a sharpening stone. *Steels* are used often—daily even—to keep an edge smooth. *Stones* are used seasonally to reestablish a knifes' edge.

2. COMBINE THE INGREDIENTS

Basic procedures are discussed in their respective chapters. Once all the ingredients are prepared, combining ingredients involves mixing and heating—what we tend to think of as the "cooking" part of cooking. This is the science part, where chemical reactions such as caramelizing, emulsifying, coagulating, rising, absorbing, and other mysteries occur.

Cooking Procedures

Listed below are common cooking procedures. Read through the list to gain a basic idea. Common sense dictates that if I understand the procedure, I can do the procedure. Remember the goal of this book: increase understanding and reduce frustration.

Cooking, like any art or science, is a discipline. It can take years to master, and it can be very complicated. Maybe I assume these procedures are simple because I am a trained chef. I may have lost my perspective on the concept of "simple." Take heart; any skill is improved by a desire to learn. This book is designed to offer you the basics and to foster a friendship between you and cooking. It is surely not designed to make you the next contestant on *Master Chef*!

- BAKE: Cook with dry heat in an oven.

- BEAT: Whip or stir in an upward and circular motion.

- BIND: Use *linkgredients* to join ingredients (see Top Ten Lists).

- BLANCH: Boil then cool food quickly in order to precook, rehydrate, or remove unwanted skin.

- BLEND: Combine two or more ingredients together.

- BOIL: Heat liquid to 212°F, until it bubbles.

- BREAD: Coat food with bread crumbs or flour mixture.

- BROIL: Cook in oven under direct heat.

- CARAMELIZE: Fry on high heat in order to brown the natural sugars in food.

- CHOP: Cut into pieces.

- COAGULATE: Thicken protein into a congealed mass.

- COAT: Cover with bread crumbs, flour, or batter when frying or baking.

- CREAM: Whip or stir foods quickly to create a fluffy and creamy consistency.

- CUT IN: Incorporate fat into flour by "cutting in" with either a pastry cutter, two knives, or by hand.

- DEGLAZE: Pour liquid onto the stuck-on residue on the bottom of a hot pan after frying, in order to create a sauce from it.

- DICE: Cut food into small square-shaped pieces.

- DILUTE: Reduce the intensity of a flavor by adding liquid.

- FLOUR: Coat food with flour.

- FOLD: Combine a whipped ingredient into denser ingredients by gently stirring upward in order to lighten texture and color.

- *FONDUE*: Means "*melted*" and is a pot of sauce used for dipping chunks of food.

- FRY: Cook in fat with direct heat. The amount of fat determines the method of frying:

    - *SAUTÉ*—fry with a little fat.

    - *PAN-FRYING*—fry with a generous amount of fat.

    - *DEEP-FRYING*—fry by immersing the food into fat.

- GARNISH: Accessorize a dish. It's the jewelry of food. Use fresh colorful herbs and sliced raw vegetables to make a dish look unified and visually appealing.

- GRATE: Shred as in grated cheese or carrots.

- GRILL: Cook over an open flame.

- KNEAD: Work bread dough to make its gluten develop, which promotes rising and gives bread its chewy texture.

- MILL: Grind raw grains or beans to make flour.

- MINCE: Cut food into very small pieces.

- MIX: Stir ingredients together until blended.

- PEEL: Remove the skin of a fruit or vegetable.

- PIT: Remove the pit of a fruit.

- PLUMP: Rehydrate or soak dried foods, until they absorb enough liquid to soften.

- PROOF: Allow the yeast to raise dough before baking.

- PUREE: Mash food into a thick paste, sauce, or soup.

- **REDUCE:** Reduce the cooking liquid by gentle boiling to intensify the flavor.

- **REHYDRATE:** Return water back into a dried ingredient through soaking.

- **RISE:** Heighten in volume through heat, moisture, and with a rising product (like yeast or baking powder).

- **ROAST:** Cook with dry heat in an oven.

- **ROLL OUT:** Thin dough for crusts by pressing with hands or using a rolling pin.

- **SAUTÉ:** Means "to jump"—frying something in a small amount of oil while stirring or tossing food.

- **SEAR:** Fry or singe a product on all sides in order to create a caramelized "crust," which seals in the flavor.

- **SHRED:** Slice into thin strips or strands.

- **SIFT:** Force flour through a screen or stir with a whip to remove lumps.

- **SIMMER:** Gently boil a sauce, soup, or food item on the stove or in the oven.

- **SKIM:** Remove undesirables—fat or foam—from the surface of food.

- **SPROUT:** Bring seeds to life through soaking and rinsing.

- **STEAM:** Cook on the stove with a small amount of water so that steam forms and cooks food quickly.

- **STIR:** Blend in a circular lifting motion.

- **STIR-FRY:** Sauté and steam concurrently.

- **WHIP:** Stir food quickly, incorporating air into it, thereby making it lighter.

- **ZEST:** Finely grate, typically with citrus rind.

When there is a range of tolerance, honor

the pansy taste buds and then keep enough

Insanity Brew around for those hard cores.

3. ADJUST THE INGREDIENTS

The reason why it is inappropriate to exactly follow a recipe is quite logical and obvious: Everyone has different tastes! Remember the two types of optional ingredients: accessory and sauce. These ingredients are in your hands.

Cooking is dynamic. Discover your family and friends' tastes and adjust the flavor to suit them. My father enjoys food so hot that it would scald a normal people's tongues and inflame their sinus passages. When I cook for him, I turn up the heat. (Of course, nothing is ever hot enough for him. He always adds crazy hot preparations with odd names like "Insanity Brew.") On the other hand, my father-in-law was raised in a household where pizza was considered spicy. This, of course, causes my father to roll off his chair and howl with laughter.

Respect your audience. When there is a range of tolerance, honor the pansy taste buds and then keep enough Insanity Brew around for those hard cores. Many people are on low-salt or low-fat diets. Adjust a recipe to accommodate the people you are serving.

My classic overseasoning tale is the *Attack of the 50-foot Tall Dressing*. You've been there. It goes something like this: I start with a little oil and vinegar in a small jar. Tasting this, I realize that it's too sour and add a bit more oil. Now it's too oily. So I add a bit of vinegar and some water to dilute the oiliness. Now the dressing is mild and bland, so I add garlic, salt and pepper. After tasting this adjustment, I realize that it's too salty, so I add more oil, vinegar, and water. Now I can't taste the garlic, so I add more and throw in a few herbs. The herbs overwhelm the flavor, so I add more vinegar. I can't cut the sour flavor unless I add a bit of sweetener, so I pour in a bit of maple syrup. Oops—now it's too sweet, so I add more water and oil. In no time, I've created a gallon of salad dressing . . . that . . . almost tastes good.

Please heed this tip! Go slowly and add ingredients prudently. You'll be glad you did.

Salads: The Tip of the Iceberg

Salads are festive combinations in marinade. Whether raw or cooked, the marinating of the ingredients makes them more palatable, with superior texture in the mouth and improved digestion in the stomach.

Salads are simple but powerful cookery. Variety is limitless, preparation is minimal, and health benefits are optimal. A salad is not confined to the lowly iceberg or the practical potato — no, indeed. Salads may be created from anything — grains, beans, even seaweed!

Salads have a marinade or *dressing*, as it is commonly known. Marinades use an acid product such as vinegar or lemon, which predigests the ingredients. It literally initiates the process of digestion by breaking down proteins. Marinating also helps combine the ingredients by helping them (literally, again) stick together. In this way, foods are, well . . . swinging . . . grooving . . . dancing, not just chopped together and tossed into a bowl.

Naked vegetables sit austerely in a bowl. *Marinated* vegetables cling romantically to one another and "marry," if you will. Do you feel the poetry? A raw piece of broccoli is a crunchy, waxy, rubbery, solitary piece. The *marinated* broccoli snaps gaily in one's mouth. It offers a melody of garlic and olive oil. It is a tangy, predigested morsel serenading your intestinal audience. That marinated broccoli has soul! Oooaaah, baby!

Following the Basic Recipe Formula, a salad is composed of:

> 1. **MAIN INGREDIENT(S)**
>
> 2. **ACCESSORY INGREDIENT(S)**
>
> 3. **SAUCE**

American salads typically use iceberg lettuce as the main ingredient. Accessories are typically "garden variety" vegetables: tomatoes, cucumbers, and onions . . . maybe carrots and peppers if one is going all out. The dressing, typically, is store-bought Italian or Thousand Island. While this at least counts for eating vegetables, it is far from definitive saladry. Unfortunately, this is the only salad that some people ever encounter. Gag me with a spoon. Where's the singing? The swinging? *The poetry*, for the love of Pete?

Hmm. Am I dancing or cooking, Susie?

Both, my dear. In people's defense, iceberg lettuce looks good on paper: firm, round, dense, and affordable. Yet it lacks in nutritional value. It supplies primarily water and sodium; therefore, it is an undesirable choice for the main ingredient in salads. Remember, that main ingredient *counts*. Use different lettuces; they offer more flavor, texture, color, and nutrition. Choose green or red leaf, romaine, or the lovely bib. Best are the mesclan mixes, now common in supermarkets.

The main ingredient in a salad, however, need not be lettuce or even a vegetable. It can be any grain, bean, or legume.

Using the BASIC RECIPE FORMULA, let's take a look at some possible ingredients:

MAIN	ACCESSORY	SAUCE
Lettuce	Vegetables	Vinegar
Sprouts	Cheese	Tamari
Lentils	Seeds: sunflower, pumpkin, sesame	Lemon
Bulgur	Nuts: almond, pecan, walnut	Oil
Couscous	Sprouts: alfalfa, clover, mung bean	Tomato
Pasta	Egg	Tahini
Beans, legumes		Miso
Grains		Yogurt
Vegetables		Mayonnaise
Fresh herbs		Herbs & spices

Now, using the Basic Recipe procedures, lets make a salad!

As with all non-recipes, I'm not telling you what to make, but I'll walk you through it. Let's start with what is available. What time of year is it? What do you have in the house? I see lentils and barley in the pantry and fresh parsley in the garden. Nice. Let's make some Lentil-Barley salad. We have onions, celery . . . oh, here are some green olives. They'll add a tangy bite. Let's keep with an Italian theme. Red peppers add vibrant color contrast to all these green and white ingredients.

Now, what will be your dressing? Check the Italian list ("International Seasonings" section). How about basil, fennel, and parsley? Good. Remember the garlic! Lentil's green and barley's white complement each other; therefore, vinaigrette is suitable. A creamy dressing might make the salad unattractive. But again, if you want creamy, it's your decision.

What about the shapes of the vegetables? Lentils and barley are small and round. If the vegetables are cut in short thin strips, it would create an interesting, complementary contrast. Or you could cut simple chunks. Let's cut the olives in cross sections to show off their pretty red pimento and add a contrasting round shape.

How do I make this salad?

→ Cook the lentils and barley separately.

→ While they are cooking, make the dressing.

→ Cut the vegetables. In a large bowl, combine the vegetables and dressing.

→ Add the lentils and barley.

→ Stir. Adjust. Chill. Serve.

Why do I cook the lentils and barley separately?

Because we cook with common sense. Cooked together, they might become mushy and grey-greenish—ick. Cooking separately retains distinct texture, color, and contrast.

You say "common sense," but I wouldn't have known that. It's not common sense to me.

I know, and it's okay. Maybe you would have cooked them together, creating dull colors and smushed textures. You would observe and retain this information for next time. Dull smushiness aside, it would still taste yummy. Pretty it up with chopped parsley and you'd saved the day. If it is *really* ugly, just add water and a touch of sweetener, heat it up, and call it soup.

TIP: Basic physics—small and hot foods absorb a marinade more rapidly. Lentils and barley are small and hot; therefore, they need less time to marinate.

You haven't told me how to cook grains or beans!

Fair enough. The next chapters cover these. I'm just walking you through one recipe. Next we'll dig into the "how" of cooking. What else?

Why make the dressing before cutting the vegetables?

Because we cook with *mise en place*. This allows the dressing's flavors to combine, mellow, ripen, awaken, marry, and bloom. Give your dressing time to develop its tastes. Even a marinade needs to marinate!

Is that why I combine the vegetables and dressing first? To allow their flavors to marry?

Yes! The vegetables are raw. Marinating allows them to boogie in the salad rather than sit stiffly like wallflowers in a bowl.

Why refrigerate this salad?

Most salads taste better cold. There are exceptions. Sample the salad both warm and cold, and then decide for yourself. Observe and retain your preference.

Some ingredients are listed as BOTH "Main" and "Accessory." How is that possible?

It depends on which role they are playing. Think of the main ingredient in a few ways: A main ingredient is what defines the recipe. A sandwich has some kind of bread and protein, frittata has eggs, and bean salad has . . . well, beans. Main ingredients are also determined by amounts. A recipe has more of the main ingredient than any other ingredients. For example, Cream of Broccoli soup has more broccoli and water (or stock) than any other ingredients. In Lentil-Barley salad, lentils and barley are the main ingredients. The veggies are the accessories, and the herbs, oil, and vinegar comprise the sauce.

Congratulations! You just made Italian Lentil-Barley salad without a recipe!

You will notice I make no reference as to amounts of ingredients. Do you live alone? Make a little. Do you run a day care? Make a lot. Is this a Mish Mash session? Be prudent. Love bean salads? Have you made this before? Go for it.

Cooking is about personal choice. The only standard is yours.

The Vegetable Rainbow

Vegetables contribute a rainbow of colors, textures, and shapes to our culinary kingdom. They offer a wealth of vitamins and minerals, which keep our body processes humming along. Vegetables are rich in water, which keeps us hydrated. They are low in calories, so you can eat a boat load of them. However, they are high in fiber. If you eat veggies by the boat load, then heed another type of load. I'm just saying. What goes down must come out, you dig?

The healthiest ways to prepare vegetables are to:

STEAM   **MARINATE**

STIR-FRY OR SAUTÉ   **EAT RAW**

STEAM

Steaming is an ideal way to prepare vegetables. Steaming leaves more nutrients intact than other heating procedures. Steaming also enhances the color of the vegetable rather than dulling it.

Basic Steaming:

→ Pour water into a pot.

→ Place cut vegetables directly into a pot or pan. Steamer tray is optimal but not necessary.

→ Cover pot. Bring water to a boil and then reduce heat to medium-high.

→ Cook vegetables until *al dente* and tender.

How much water?

A bit. Never cover vegetables with water when steaming. The water should rise to meet the veggies about a quarter of their way. This sounds weird, I know. Ideally, you want to use enough water so that the steam produced will cook the product by the time the water evaporates. When the water's gone, the veggies are done.

How should vegetables be cut?

Basic physics apply: The larger the size and harder the vegetable, the longer the cooking time. If you are making a salad or just short on time, create smaller cuts. If you are steaming veggies as a side dish, larger cuts are appealing. Asparagus, for instance, should be steamed whole. Baby vegetables are especially lovely steamed whole. Broccoli and cauliflower look attractive with full florets and part of the stalk. Steamed leafy greens are just a big ol' lump of green, so chop roughly or leave smaller greens whole.

Basic physics apply: The larger the size and harder the vegetable, the longer the cooking time.

What is al dente?

Al dente translates as, "to the bite." It means cooking a vegetable until biting down on it breaks the bitten piece off effortlessly. There is the tiniest of snaps as the food resists the bite. Steamed vegetables should not be crunchy or mushy. The *snap* is perfection. Consider *al dente* a masticating *Bing.*

What's the difference between steaming and boiling?

The differences are in the amount of water used and the part of the water that is involved in cooking. In boiling, the product is submerged and surrounded by liquid. With steaming, the product sits mostly above the water, surrounded by steam. Boiling is also more invasive in terms of destroying nutrients.

Why do people boil vegetables, then?

I give up, why? Okay, seriously, I guess people boil veggies because they are taught to do so. Or they buy precooked frozen bags of veggies that are prepared by submerging them into boiling water. Longer-cooking vegetables like potatoes, turnips, or beets are generally boiled due to their size and density. In general, steaming is actually easier, takes less time, uses less water, and wastes less heat. It's a winny-win-winster.

To REHEAT STEAMED VEGETABLES, boiling is preferable:

→ Boil enough water to submerge the portion.

→ Place vegetables in boiling water briefly—about a minute.

→ Remove with tongs, slotted spoon, or fork, or drain into a strainer.

→ Reuse the cooking liquid.

STIR-FRY OR SAUTÉ

This method awakens the most flavors in vegetables thanks to its caramelizing technique. *Sauté*—meaning "to jump"—is frying that involves motion. Compared to pan-frying, where food sits in oil, sautéed food is busy—tossed, stirred, rolled, and pushed—jumping in the pan. All frying, whether it is stir-frying, sautéing, or pan-frying, allows food to gently sear and its sugary juices to caramelize. Thus, the flavor is superior to steaming, especially for high-sugar or long-cooking veggies like carrots, broccoli, celery, and onions.

What kind of oil is best for frying?

Use high-heat oils such as grapeseed, peanut, safflower, or canola. These oils retain their nutrients at high heats, compared with low-burning fats like olive oil and butter.

How much oil do I use?

Use enough oil to gently coat the vegetables and not so much that they soak in it.

Stir-frying and **sautéing** use less oil than pan-frying, as the frequent motion prevents sticking or burning. In sautéing or stir-frying, no extra oil is in the pan; oil just coats the product. Less oil and frying translate into a healthier meal.

Pan-frying is the opposite; the key is to keep the product stationary while it fries. This allows the skin to sear or turn golden brown. Picture hash-brown potatoes, burgers, and eggplant parmesan. The trick is in allowing them to sit still while they fry. Leave them alone; they're busy becoming delicious! Because of this technique, pan-frying uses more oil; the bottom of the product is surrounded with a layer of oil. Some of the oil absorbs into the food product. Delicious, yes! But, healthy? Less.

BASIC FRYING RULE

Hot Pan ☞ **Hot Oil** ☞ **Hot Product**

How do I know when the oil is ready for frying?

→ Heat your pan.

→ Heat the oil until it *just* starts to smoke:

The oil should "thin" in the pot.

Watch the oil—you will notice this—the oil appears to spread or thin out.

→ Add vegetables in order of slowest to quickest cooking.

On what heat do I fry?

Medium-high heat. Watch the heat and oil at this point, and stir the vegetables frequently. If veggies are singing too loudly, reduce the heat. If they're inactive, turn it up. When stirring, note if they begin sticking. If they are, add a little oil or a splash of water.

Be in control. Use your senses. If there is too much noise, too much smoke, if food smells burnt, if oil pops up and burns you, or if you're just starting to freak out, then reduce the heat. (Are we still talking about cooking?)

TIP: If product begins sticking and smoking, REMOVE the pan from the heat for a few seconds, turn the heat down a bit, add a little water, and return to the heat, stirring well.

What's the difference between sautéing and stir-frying?

Stir-frying is a combination of sautéing and steaming. Sautéing uses only oil, whereas stir-frying uses oil *and* cooking liquids like water or stock. Sautéing mainly cooks the outer layers. Stir-frying has the benefit of steaming to complete cooking. If you try to sauté a large piece of vegetable, you wind up with something that looks cooked but is raw and crunchy inside. Small pieces can be sautéed; larger pieces are best stir-fried.

When do I add the liquid when stir-frying?

After a bit. Add liquid when the vegetables have sautéed a few minutes, depending upon the size and type of vegetable.

How much liquid?

Not much. We want to gently steam the veggies, not boil them. Start with a couple of spoonfuls, simmer, and add more if necessary. Do not add too much liquid, or the vegetables will become mushy and dull in color.

TIP: Add tamari as part of the liquid. It adds salty flavor and nutrients, complementing plain water in stir-frying.

What do you do after adding liquid?

Stir, bring to a boil, reduce to a simmer, and cover the pan. Covering contains the steam and forms pressure, which minimizes cooking time and retains nutrition. **This is a common technique: BRING TO A BOIL AND REDUCE TO A SIMMER.**

Using this technique keeps food in the safety range and conserves energy by propelling food's cooking time. You will use this technique in stir-frying and cooking soups and sauces.

I've used liquid in sautéing. Was I stir-frying?

Aah, good point. Yes and no. If the vegetables needed more cooking time then yes, you were stir-frying. But you might have been performing another important cooking technique—DEGLAZING—which is adding liquid to the hot pan after the product is cooked.

What does DEGLAZING do? It looks important, because you typed it in ALL CAPS.

You are correct. Deglazing is a biggie. What it does is grab up all those great, caramelized bits on the bottom of the pan and magically turn them into sweet, delicious sauce. It's so cool.

Deglazing is that fancy loud thing that chefs do to impress us.

Adding liquid to fried food or sticky juices makes a loud sizzle and causes a billowing puff of steam. When chefs use alcohol to deglaze a pan, huge flames flare up, impressing and scaring patrons. On a less sexy note, deglazing also halts the cooking process so that food is not overcooked. And while deglazing with alcohol flames is particularly impressive, it can cause hair and house fires. Please, do not try this at home; deglazing with water works just fine.

In terms of all these methods, it sounds like size matters.

Absolutely.

Here's a little quiz.

How long will vegetables take to cook?

Well, I guess it would depend on how big they are cut. Right?

Right! It also depends on the density of the veggie—whether it is watery or solid.

How would I know that?

If you think about it and use common sense, you likely know more than you give yourself credit. Which is more watery or less solid—carrot or zucchini?

Zucchini?

Yep. So, which one would likely take less time to cook?

Zucchini?

Yep. Unless what?

Well . . . unless you're cooking an entire zucchini versus a small dice of carrot.

Bingo! Nicely played.

Included next is a vegetable cooking chart, which offers the spectrum of quicker-to-slower cooking veggies.

VEGETABLE COOKING CHART (IN MINUTES)

Quick Vegetables under 10	Medium Vegetables 10–15	Slow Vegetables 15–30
Peppers	Corn	Potatoes
Zucchini	Cauliflower	Turnip
Tender leafy greens: spinach, chard	Green beans	Squash
Garlic*	Mushrooms	Tomatoes
	Brassica family: broccoli, cabbage, brussels sprouts	Carrots, onion, celery
	Hardy leafy greens: kale, collards	Garlic*
	Garlic*	

*Garlic can be sauted at any time.

MARINATE

To marinate is to absorb sauce into food. Marinating is simple because the food does all the work. Introduce the ingredients, and physics takes it from there. The key essential-main-absolutely-necessary ingredient for successful marinating is time. Allow food to sit at least one day, preferably more. Marinating is a ceremony, and all ceremonies take time.

What are some examples of marinating vegetables?

First the obvious ones: olives, pickles, capers, mushrooms, peppers, and any other cured or pickled product. Salads marinate their ingredients: potato salads, cucumber salads, Cole slaws . . . picture a salad bar. How about that broccoli salad with carrots, raisins, and mayonnaise? Marinated. Less obvious, but consider the chutney and salsa. *Marinated!*

Are there foods that I can marinate quickly?

Yes, and some are better with less marinating. Lettuce salads and cucumber salads grow soggy overnight. This is where "marinating" a salad is referred to as "dressing" a salad. But in the most technical sense, it is the same process—the same ingredients are used with the same procedures. The only variable is time.

The key essential-main-absolutely-necessary ingredient for successful marinating is Time.

EAT 'EM RAW

Raw foods have vital force and living energy. Most vegetables taste good raw, whereas some need to develop their flavors with marinating, fermenting, or cooking.

Some people avoid raw vegetables, especially whole, because they find a big hunk of raw broccoli or carrot unappealing. I tend to agree. There is a time for whole veggies, such as pulling a carrot out of the garden, wiping off the excess dirt, and eating it on the spot. Or yanking an apple off the tree, shining it clean on your dirty shirt, and chomping away. But if you leave whole vegetables in your refrigerator, then that is where and how they'll remain.

Simply cutting raw vegetables improves their flavor and texture. Grating, slicing, or chopping releases their juices, and juice is where the flavor lives. The texture improves, too. A grated carrot is chewier than a big ol' honka stick. There are times that call for carrot sticks and long stalks of celery; take your Sunday Bloody Mary, for example. But for the most part, cutting is the way to go.

Please remember that these are guidelines, not commandments. Always take your own tastes into account. My sons, for instance, enjoy chomping away on whole red peppers as one would an apple. Creed, from *The Office*, once ate a whole raw potato. You wanna maw into a big ol' honka carrot? It's your kitchen, chef.

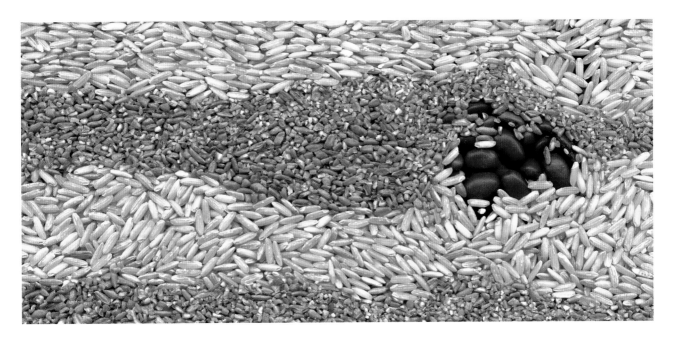

Amazing Grains and Simple Sugars

Grains are the main food source in the human diet, comprising approximately half of all food consumed. Whole grains are high in fiber and complex carbohydrates. Carbohydrates are to the body what gasoline is to an engine. A car runs on gasoline, but gasoline needs "nutrients" to burn. A body cannot burn carbohydrate without a little help. It needs protein, minerals, vitamins, enzymes, oxygen, and other nutrients to properly convert the carbohydrate into a form that can be assimilated into the body's cells. This is why Doritos and Saltines do not qualify as grains. They do not supply the nutrients needed for fuel consumption.

> **Nature knew exactly what she was doing when she created the whole grain.**

Nature knew exactly what she was doing when she created the whole grain. Whole grains contain all the nutrients necessary to properly assimilate that particular grain's carbohydrate. In fact, all the nutrients contained in any whole food are those nutrients needed to properly assimilate that particular whole food. That is why we eat whole foods. Nature has researched all the chemistry for us; we simply eat her intricate science.

In their natural state, carbohydrates are complex—made up of long sugar chains, which the body breaks down slowly. This ensures a consistent and reasonable release of sugar into the bloodstream. From there, sugar is transported into cells to use as energy, sustain our attention, feed friendly bacteria, and generally maintain the body's metabolism.

If a carbohydrate is refined, it is known as a *simple* sugar. Simple sugars are . . . simple! Simple to burn, that is. They are so simple that the body doesn't need to do anything— break down or convert—for them to be absorbed into the bloodstream. The problem lies in the amount of sugar being absorbed into the bloodstream. Complex carbohydrates release steadily as the body carefully monitors its sugar level and converts starch to sugar as it is needed. Simple sugars are the *Fast and the Furious*—raging rampantly, flooding the bloodstream, and dangerously raising blood sugar levels. Picture a damn bursting. Your body is the small town in the valley below. Plus, sugar is acidic—highly acidic. Too much sugar in the blood can cause acidosis. If you have any doubts as to its potential health hazard, ask any diabetic about acidosis; it can be fatal. So, not only is the town inundated with flooding water, but the water is polluted.

Where do simple sugars come from?

Simple sugars are created from the refining process of grains: removing the bran and germ (nutritious outer layers). The primary component—the white starch or simple sugar—is then cooked and ground; often it is bleached and preserved. Simple sugars are extractions from corn and sugar cane primarily. But one can isolate simple sugars from most anything that contains high amounts of sugar, such as honey, fruits, and tree syrups, like maple.

Why do we have simple sugars, if they are so dangerous to our health?

Why do we produce and sell anything, if it's dangerous to our health? The answer is simple. Simple sugars don't spoil. The more refined a food is, the longer its shelf life. Refining a food is a matter of economics, benefitting neither the food nor its consumer. The one who benefits is the stockholder, and if he's smart, he's not consuming his own product.

Do you recall the notorious quote by tobacco company executive, RJ Reynolds?

"We don't smoke that [garbage]. We just sell it. We reserve the right to smoke for the young, the poor, the black and stupid."

Just because something is sold widely and accepted culturally doesn't mean that it is offered in the public's best interest. It's usually the other way around. Good health is subversive. You have to work, research, defend, and sometimes fight for your right to be healthy. Health is a sacred gift that we discard like a bag of McDonald's garbage out of a car window. (I use that particular metaphor because when I was eighteen, I did that. I've regretted it ever since.)

What are some forms of refined grains?

White flour and its products: pasta, frozen entrees, junk cereals, and pastries. Basically any packaged food found in a supermarket is a refined food. Check labels carefully. Product labels should state "whole wheat" or "whole grain" as their primary ingredient. Even if a product claims to contain "whole grain" (e.g., whole wheat bagels, 7-grain bread, etc.), the main ingredient may still be white flour. The label might also say, "wheat flour." This does not necessarily mean "whole wheat." Legally, "wheat flour" can be white flour with artificial color. Unless it says *whole* wheat or *whole* grain flour, assume that its primary ingredient is refined white flour.

Good health is subversive. You have to work, research, defend, and sometimes fight for your right to be healthy.

Other than grains, are there any refined products I ought to avoid?

Any refined product is under suspicion, and some are major culprits. Refined oils are less nutritious and host preservatives and bleaches. Bad enough, right? Almost. Hydrogenated oils win the prize for most damaging oil refinery toward our systems.

Hydrogenated or trans-fat oils are oils that go through chemical manipulation: extra hydrogen atoms are forced onto the long fatty molecular chains. The new *isomer* (similar chemical compound but restructured) becomes twisted through a process called "trans-isomerization"—thus the name, trans-fats.

What's the benefit in doing this?

This twisted trans-isomerization and hydrogenation procedure is performed because people like to spread things on bread.

How's that??

Once upon a time, back in the 1950s, butter got a bad rap. It was scapegoated for causing heart attacks, obesity, and other cardiovascular problems. A logical alternative would have been to switch to olive and other vegetable oils. But, no . . . people (North Americans) liked *spreading* something on their bread. *Dip* one's bread in oil?

What are you, some kind of barbaric Mediterranean savage? Oh, dear, no. Also, we prefer pies and cookies to those ruffian puff pastry concoctions like *Baklava*, which nicely tolerate liquid oil. Pies call on solid fat to create those flaky crusts we crave. Oh, yes; one's bread must *spread,* and one's crusts must *flake.*

Food that is advertised as "zero trans-fats" or "trans-fat-free" is most likely anything but.

In order to both satisfy public demand and avoid killing people, we needed a vegetable oil that was solid at room temperature. So, economists and marketers responded the way they always do: by employing scientists to figure it out. Make a solution, they implored. And those crafty scientists did—by inventing hydrogenation. Vegetable oil became solid at room temperature, and suddenly margarine and Crisco were available in every supermarket. Sweet ads displaying lovely young homemakers wearing brightly colored aprons describing how they could spread bread and fry foods and create flaky pie crusts with non-saturated fats inundated Good Housekeeping magazines. Vegetable oil was solid at room temperature! Huzzah! This changed everything. This dandy fat miracle could do everything butter did, but since it was vegetable—not animal—all would be sparred their nasty little heart attacks.

Except that this didn't happen. What happened was that no one realized that in hydrogenating an oil, it stops being an oil—well, an edible oil, anyway. It becomes something more like a plastic and burns in a similar way. Ever try burning plastic? What happens? Mhm. Now picture that effect in your body. The "fat" molecules in hydrogenated products break down less efficiently than the regular, nonmanipulated products. Globules of this plastic fat remain in your blood vessels and intestines. These cause blockages, stick to walls, and contribute to stroke, heart attack, and colonic diseases, such as diverticulitis and IBS.

This atrocious revelation is not big news. It is common practice in our culture to create first and consider the implications later. If you don't believe me, just go and watch yourself some *Jurassic Park* movies. That'll put a learnin' on ya.

One more horrid revelation regarding hydrogenated oils: Food that is advertised as "zero trans-fats" or "trans-fat-free" is most likely anything but. Current USFDA laws allow a product to list ingredients in increments of .5 grams per serving size—namely hydrogenated oils. So let's say a product contains .49 grams of hydrogenated fat per serving. It could be legally listed as 0 grams of fat per serving. If you're porking away on half a bag of potato chips, you may be eating a few grams of the plastic poison.

A few grams doesn't seem like so much. I mean, how bad can it be?

Several respected mainstream authorities have strong opinions about this and have issued warnings:

- The U.S. Government's recommendation in its *Dietary Guidelines for Americans 2005* is ***"keep trans-fatty acid consumption as low as possible."***

- In June 2006, the American Heart Association (AHA) issued its "2006 Diet and Lifestyle Recommendations." The AHA recommends that your daily intake of trans-fats be limited to 1 percent of total calories, which is equivalent to roughly **2 to 2.5 grams of trans-fat per day**.

- Institute of Medicine recommends we keep our intake of trans fats to **"as near zero as possible."** (http://pubs.cas.psu.edu/freepubs/pdfs/uk093.pdf)

When subversive health nuts and mainstream experts agree, you know you got a nasty product. The vote is in. Hydrogenated oils are bad news. Stay away.

What products should I buy?

First and foremost, buy organic whole grains: wheat, rice, millet, barley, oats, and rye. Next, buy processed, whole organic grains: whole grain pastas, rolled oats, corn grits, and grain cereals. Buy whole grain flours.

Purchase unrefined, organic oils. Choose cold-pressed or expeller-pressed oils. Otherwise, oils are extracted through high heat and chemical processes, which, while more efficient, destroy nutrient density. Oils, grains, and sugars are all turned into "white" empty products, void of any nutritional benefits.

TIP: Palm or coconut oils are outstanding vegetarian substitutes for either hydrogenated fats or butter.

☞ **Remember the *Paycheck Principle*:** Your job is to be alive and healthy. Part of that job description requires you to eat a few meals every day. You get paid for the amount of nutrition you receive. If you don't receive nutrients in your food, you're not doing your job and you don't get paid. And sooner or later, you're gonna get fired.

TIP: Refrigerate your grain products and oils or store them in a cool dry place. Whole grains have nutrients and natural oils, so they will spoil. Since organic foods are not sprayed with pesticides, they are likely to attract bugs. Cool storage reduces these issues.

For maximum nutritional benefits, grind your own flour or purchase locally milled flour. It is the freshest, most nutritious, and best tasting flour money can buy. Personally I do not grind my own flour. But I have in the past, and I've been surprised by the difference. One can use a blender or handheld mill—available in kitchen and hardware stores. I know the crazybusy contingency will twist and shout on this one, but if you want to get paid the big bucks on nutrition, try it.

Cooking Grains

SLOW GRAINS	PASTA
QUICK GRAINS	ROLLED OATS & GRITS
COUSCOUS & BULGUR	POPCORN

Each section lists the ratio of liquid to grain.

Why ratios and not amounts?

Ratios are . . . well, ratios. They offer more freedom to cook the amount you want:

- 1 CUP rice = 2 CUPS of liquid

- 1 GALLON of rice = 2 GALLONS of liquid

- 1 GRECIAN URNS of rice = 2 GRECIAN URNS of liquid

- 1 WHEEL BARROW of rice = 2 WHEEL BARROWS of liquid

- 1 BATHTUB of rice = 2 BATHTUBS of liquid

I guess you get the point.

SLOW GRAINS: RICE, BARLEY, WHEAT BERRIES

RATIO: 1 part GRAIN to 2 parts LIQUID

→ Pour grain into a pot.

→ Rinse the grain a few times.

→ Add liquid and cover pot.

→ Bring to a boil and then reduce to a low simmer.

→ Cook until done.

→ Stir with a fork to fluff or separate the grain.

How do I rinse the grain?

After placing your grain in a pot, fill the pot with water. Swish the grain around with your hands. Allow the grain to settle to the bottom. Slowly drain the water. Repeat a couple of times.

TIP: For desserts, sushi, or casseroles, you *want* mushy clumpy rice! Rinse grains *once*, only to clean, while retaining the starch. The result is a stickier, gooier cereal-type of grain, useful for combining other ingredients.

What does rinsing the grain do?

Rinsing accomplishes two things:

- It removes any dirt, stones, and bugs that may have been packaged with the grain.
- It removes some of the starch so that the grain cooks up fluffy and separated, rather than mushy and clumpy.

How long do I cook grains?

Cook them until they're done. Check the grain after 20 minutes and then every few minutes thereafter, until you like its consistency.

What kind of liquid is good?

Stocks are great, and water is fine. It depends on how you use the grain. If you plan to use it in desserts, you might cook the grain in apple cider or nut milk. Experiment, observe, and retain.

TIP: Liquid amounts may vary. When the liquid is absorbed, check the grains. If they are not yet done, add a bit more liquid.

QUICK GRAINS: QUINOA, TEFF, AMARANTH

RATIO: 1 part GRAIN to 2 parts LIQUID

→ Bring water to a boil.

→ Add grain.

→ Return to a boil and reduce to a simmer.

→ Cook until done.

These tiny, bead-like grains are highly nutritious, low in fat, and have a delicious, nutty-sweet flavor. They cook much faster than rice, for a quick alternative. Check them after 10 minutes.

COUSCOUS (WHEAT PASTA BALLS) & BULGUR (CRACKED WHEAT)

RATIO: 1 part GRAIN to 2 parts LIQUID

→ Place couscous or bulgur into a bowl.

→ Bring water to a boil. Pour boiling water over couscous/bulgur.

→ Stir and cover for 5 minutes.

Couscous is tiny, precooked pasta balls made from durum semolina—a type of wheat. Bulgur is cracked parboiled wheat. They are rehydrated rather than cooked.

PASTA

RATIO: 1 part PASTA to 4 parts WATER

→ Bring water to a *rolling* boil.

→ Add oil and salt.

→ Add pasta. Stir.

→ Boil rapidly until done.

→ Drain and rinse.

→ Oil the pasta.

- Dry pasta cooks in 5–10 minutes, depending on shapes, sizes, and grain.

- Fresh pasta cooks in 2–5 minutes.

Check the package for time suggestions. Always check the pasta as it cooks.

What is a rolling boil?
The water boils so rapidly that bubbles appear to roll in the water.

Why do we need a rolling boil to cook pasta?
A rolling boil prevents clumping and keeps the pasta pieces separated. When pasta is cooked on low heat, it tends to congeal and winds up as a gloppy mass.

TIP: COVER THE POT

You'll save about 10 minutes (and conserve energy!) when you cover pots to boil liquid.

Why do we add oil and salt to the rolling water?

These further prevent the pasta from lumping together. If you have vigorous boil, they are optional.

How much oil and salt?

Oh, you. Depends on how much pasta you're making. If you're making a bag of pasta, then use about a small spoonful of both.

How do I add the pasta?

ALL AT ONCE! Prevent uneven cooking—soggy noodles in one bite and crunchy noodles in another. After adding pasta to water, stir briskly to avoid lumping.

How do I know when the pasta is done?

Pasta is normally cooked *al dente.* Pasta should "nibble you back" as you bite into it, creating resistance. Pasta should never be mushy; it should have an attitude.

Be careful about undercooking. After biting into it, look at the bitten end. Does any part look white or floury? Do you need to tug the pasta a bit to bite through it? If so, it is undercooked. When it is *al dente*, a simple nibble will separate the pasta end, and there will be no "white in the bite." And again, taste counts. Undercooked pasta tastes raw. Overcooked is mushy and tastes like water. *Al dente* pasta is snappy and fresh. You'll know.

> TIP: An old cook's tale claims that spaghetti is properly cooked when a strand sticks upon throwing it at a wall. I have found this to be usually true.

Why rinse and oil pasta after cooking?

Rinsing removes excess starch, which prevents lumping. When you oil the pasta, add just enough to coat the pieces. Then lift the oiled pasta up and down—like tossing a salad—to help distribute the oil, cool the pasta, and reduce carry-over cooking.

ROLLED OATS AND GRITS

RATIO: 1 part GRAIN to 2 parts WATER

→ Bring water to a boil.

→ Add oats or grits and return to a boil.

→ Reduce heat and gently cook until done, stirring constantly.

→ Remove from heat.

→ Allow carry-over cooking.

What are grits?

Grits are tiny chopped pieces of raw or pre-cooked grain. They are ground smaller in size than couscous or bulgur but larger than flour. They have a nice consistency for breakfast cereals. Soy, corn, wheat, and oats are common. Wheat grits are sold as cracked wheat; oat grits are steel cut oats. Products such as Cream of Wheat, rye or oat bran are versions of grits.

POPCORN

→ Heat pot on high heat.

→ Cover the bottom of a pot with oil.

→ Sprinkle a layer of popcorn.

→ Cover. Wait and listen for popping sounds.

→ Reduce heat to medium-high.

→ Shake the pot *continuously* on the burner until the popping stops.

→ Remove from heat. Let sit a few minutes to make sure corn has stopped popping.

How much oil do I need?

Add just enough oil and just enough popcorn to cover the bottom of a pot.

What shall I season it with?

Salt alone is great. For a cheesy flavor, try nutritional yeast or Spike.

GRAIN COOKING CHART (IN MINUTES)

Quick Grains (5–10)	Grains (10–20)	Slow Grains (20–40)
Pasta	Quinoa	Rice
Couscous	Teff	Barley
Bulgur	Amaranth	Wheat
Popcorn	Millet	Rye
	Grits	Whole oats
	Rolled oats	Buckwheat or kasha
	Rolled barley	
	Steel cut oats	

Tables are guidelines. Cook food until it is done.

The Magical Fruit

Beans are the foundation of the kitchen: nutritious, high in fiber, low in fat, and packed with protein. They are the unsung heroes and best-kept secrets in terms of adding health to your diet. They are also super-duper afford-able. But they do come with a cost.

Most beans contain two starches, which are connected by a special link that is not normally broken down in the human intestine. Meat eaters or people not used to eating beans tend to house bacteria in the large intestines, which break down the link between these starches. They convert the starches into nitrogen, carbon dioxide, and hydrogen—the main components of what we commonly refer to as "gas."

Can I "de-gas" beans?
Gas can be reduced, but not eliminated. Fortunately, there are three easy ways to prevent at least *some* gas: soak, sprout, and seaweed.

SOAKING METHOD:

→ Place beans in a pot and cover with water. Soak for a few hours or, if possible, overnight.

→ Drain this water before cooking. The gas-making starches will begin to leech out into the soaking water.

→ Bring the beans to a boil and reduce to a simmer. As the beans boil, foam forms on the surface of the water. Skim the foam to further reduce gas.

→ Cook until done.

TIP: Do not use the soaking water (fart juice) for cooking liquid; just compost it.

Sprouting is a more effective means of de-gassing beans. Sprouting is the act of bringing a seed to life. As the sprouted seed "awakens," chemical changes occur. First, proteins and B vitamins are initiated—nutrients necessary to building life. As the sprout begins this dynamic process, it needs energy, so it utilizes its own starches, including the gas-producing culprits. The starch is converted into burnable sugars, which supply the energy for the sprout to grow.

SPROUTING METHOD:

NOTE: Sprouting for raw consumption is slightly different ("Wild Things" chapter).

→ Soak beans in water, overnight.

→ Drain the water and rinse the beans.

→ Rinse a few times during the day.

→ The next day, they are sufficiently sprouted for cooking.

→ Bring the beans to a boil, and reduce to a simmer. As the beans boil, foam forms on the surface of the water. Skim the foam, to further reduce gas.

→ Cook until done.

What if I don't have time to soak beans?

Another way to de-gas beans is to add seaweed. Seaweeds, rich in minerals, are natural tenderizers. They predigest or break down proteins and carbohydrates that cause gas. Add seaweed to beans while soaking and cooking.

What kind of seaweed should I use?

Common types are Kombu, Dulse, Kelp, or Wakame.

NOTE: Even if you use seaweed, still soak or sprout beans if possible. Plan to cook beans the day before you need them.

Are there beans that do not need to soak?

Yes. Small beans such as Aduki, Mung, lentils, and split peas may be cooked dry. Choose these if you have no time to soak. Just be sure to add seaweed!

How long do smaller beans cook?

Cooking beans varies from 30 minutes to hours, depending on size and soaking time. Cook food until it is done. If a bean is hard or "chewy," it is not ready. If it dissolves in the water or begins to peel, it is overdone.

Beans, beans, the magical fruit.
The more you soak, the less you toot!

Stone Soup

What is the difference between a salad and a soup? Water. If that seems simple, it is. Does it seem too simple? Recall our Italian Lentil-Barley salad. Add water. You just made Italian Lentil Barley soup!

How much water?

It depends. You like your soup thick or thin?

Susie, come on. A little help here.

Okay. How about this: about 2 to 1, liquid to ingredients. Use less liquid when ingredients are precooked (leftover grains and beans). The liquid should cover the ingredients at least. But you'll decide the ratio, and it can change every time.

What are the main ingredients in soup?

Let's look at a few examples:

1. **CREAM OF BROCCOLI?** BROCCOLI AND LIQUID.

2. **CLAM CHOWDER?** CLAMS AND LIQUID.

3. **MINESTRONE?** BEANS, NOODLES, AND LIQUID.

. . . and the accessories?

Remember the story of *Stone Soup*? Here's my No Recipe version:

❧   ❧   ❧

A beggar is penniless and hungry. He comes upon a house. He reaches down and picks up a stone in the yard, approaches the front door, and knocks on it. A woman approaches. "Who's there?" she asks.

"Good evening, Ma'am. I am a wayward soul, traveling without food, clothing, or money. However, I possess a stone—a *magical* stone. By simply placing the stone into a pot of water, I can produce the most delicious soup you have ever tasted. If you like, I would be happy to show you how it works, thereby creating a magnificent meal for your supper."

"That is most interesting! I should like to see this. Do come in!"

The woman invites the man inside. She brings out her large cauldron and fills it with water. She places the cauldron on the stove and brings the water to a boil. The man throws the stone into the caldron. *Splash!* The stone makes a cheery sound and sprays them gently as it hits the water. "Now we wait!" he exclaims.

After a couple minutes the man declares, "My, what a lovely soup we shall soon have. I should not like to impose upon you longer than necessary. If you have a couple potatoes handy, we could add them to the soup, only to hasten its thickening."

"What a clever idea!" she replies. A few minutes elapse. The man observes, "Well, look at those fine carrots in the corner there, growing their tops and becoming hairy. What a shame to have them go rotten. Why not toss them into the soup?"

"A wise suggestion, good sir!" she replies. A few more minutes elapse. The man suggests, "You know what goes well with carrot and potato? The rich flavor of onion, that's for sure. Yes, some onion would make the soup grand, indeed."

"Why, certainly!" the woman replies. They continue chatting about soups and stews. He remarks, "What is soup without a fine bone? Preferably one with a good lot of fat on it."

"I have the perfect bone!" cries the woman, rushing off towards the icebox. Next, the man concludes, "And to top it off, some herbs and spices—as important to a soup as a conductor is to an orchestra."

"How delightful a metaphor!" shrieks the woman, tossing salt and garlic gaily into the cauldron.

Soon the soup is finished. The man and woman sit down to a steamy bowl. "How I love a couple slices of warm bread slathered with fresh butter to complement my soup."

"But of course!" chimes the woman. "Where are my manners?! Would you care for some wine?"

"Another perfect complement to this lovely soup," he smiles, graciously.

They eat the meal. It is, indeed, a magnificent soup. Afterwards, the man kindly thanks the woman for her hospitality and makes off down the road. Abruptly the door opens, and the woman runs after the man, calling out, "Wait! You forgot your magic stone!!"

"And so I have! Dear me, I wouldn't want to lose this precious parcel! Warm thanks extend to you and your hospitality. Good night!"

The man, whistling, tosses the stone over his shoulder as he continues down the road.

      ⁊   ⁊   ⁊

What are the main ingredients? Water and stone.

What are the accessory ingredients? Anything lying around the house beginning to rot. That's soup!

It doesn't take magic to make a soup, just a couple of basic ingredients. However, you may not have Italian-Lentil Barley salad ready on hand to simply add water and create a soup.

So, let's start with the stone.

Making Soup from Scratch

My mom is the true pioneer of recipe-free cooking in our family. She invented compost soup. Compost soup involved cleaning out the freezer. Mom would dump several containers into a pot, heat them up, and taste. Whatever flavor they most resembled, she would accentuate with additional seasoning. The results were a clean freezer and hearty stew for supper.

Whether you are making soup from stone, salad, or compost, it is handy to understand some basic soup-cooking procedures. Let us begin with some basic ingredients:

LIQUID	GRAINS & BEANS
VEGETABLES	THICKENING

LIQUID

It is a soup; therefore, it needs liquid. Stock is superior to water for flavor and nutrition. Use stock when available.

What is stock?

Stock is water infused with vegetable, bones, and other flavors. Stock is like vegetable tea, if you will. When I refer to "cooking liquid," that is the simplest form of stock: the broth that remains after steaming vegetables, for example.

So, liquid means stock?

I reference the term "liquid" and interchange it with water. Basically, "liquid" refers to the replacement of water. It does not refer to the cooking oil and liquid condiments in a recipe (vinegar), even though technically, oil and vinegar are liquids. When you see "liquid," think "stock."

How do I make stock?

→ Place vegetable scraps into a pot. Fill with water.

→ Bring to a boil and reduce to a simmer.

→ Strain the stock.

→ Use right away or cool and store for later.

How long do I cook stock?

How long you got? 30–60 minutes is fine. Filling a large pot with water and letting it slowly reduce all day is best. Even if you only had five minutes, that liquid would still be better than plain water.

If you don't have time to cook or aren't around to watch it boil, you can still make stock. Add water to scraps and let the mixture sit. Some of the flavor and nutrients will leech out or infuse, like tea. Then strain the scraps and use the stock.

What are vegetable scraps?

These are all the ends, leaves, skins, and bits of vegetable that are usually thrown away or composted. To name a few:

✔ Onion and garlic skins

✔ Celery stalks

✔ Potato peelings

✔ Carrot stubs

✔ Parsley stems

Generally, if it is part of a vegetable, throw it into the pot. Make stock first, and then feed the animals or compost bin.

Are there vegetable scraps to avoid?

YES!

✔ The leaves of celery stalks create bitter flavor.

✔ The Brassica family (broccoli, cabbage, and turnips) create strong, sulfur-like flavor.

Use brassica scraps when making brassica soups. Otherwise, cook with discretion or avoid.

☞ **NEVER COOK OR EAT THE LEAVES OF NIGHTSHADE PLANTS:**
Potato, Tomato, Eggplant, or Pepper. The leaves contain toxic substances.

Do I season a stock?

No. Stock is the base. The soup will be seasoned later. An exception is when you'd like a darker, richer stock. The way to achieve this is with "burning" onions.

"Burning" onions for stock:

→ Slice an onion in half. Keep the skin on!

→ Place in a lightly greased pan on high heat.

→ "Burn" the onion: Cook it until it is dark brown on one side.

→ Add the burned onion to the stock.

NOTE: "Burning" is just a jazzy culinary term that chefs use to describe this technique. This is basically caramelizing an onion. Do not be shy about the burning; cook that onion well.

Why am I keeping the skin on the onion?

Onion skins add flavor and color to the stock.

Sheesh. Now I'm making stock every time I have scraps?

Naaw. One more thing about stock; don't worry too much about it. Cook it when you have time. Don't fret that every soup you prepare must have stock as its cooking liquid. That is perfectionist thinking, and perfection is most certainly NOT one of the seven virtues of cooking!

When you feel like making stock, make it. It is worth the extra effort but ONLY if you have the time, enjoy doing it, and can appreciate the nutritional benefits. A great compromise is to use liquids from cooking vegetables, beans, and grains. Just store them in the fridge. When you have a full jar, you might make a soup. Easy-peasy.

I generally don't make sweet stock for fruit soups. You go right ahead. The cooking procedure would be the same, but use sweet scraps such as apple cores, citrus rinds, and mushy berries. Omit banana peels, please.

One more thing about stock: Don't worry too much about it.

VEGETABLES

All kinds, one kind, it's up to you. The only rule is to add them in order of their cooking time. Sauté soup veggies, for optimal flavor. .

How long do they take to cook?

Hey. We covered this in the veggie section. *You can do this.* Let's start with some common sense.

Which takes longer to cook: potatoes or spinach?
> **Potatoes?**

Right. So then, which vegetable would you sauté first?
> **Potatoes?**

Correct!

What kind of oil do I use to sauté the vegetables?

Use high-heat oils, such as grapeseed, safflower, or canola. These oils do not lose their nutrients as easily as low-heat oils, such as olive or sunflower.

How much oil?

Use just enough oil to coat the vegetables for even sautéing—Same method as cooking vegetables on their own.

HONOR THE FRY RULE

Hot Pan ☞ **Hot Oil** ☞ **Hot Product**

How long do I sauté the vegetables?

Sauté vegetables for only a few minutes in order to caramelize them. Caramelizing is easy to spot: Notice your veggies transform. They will brown. They will smell good. The onions and celery become translucent. Fear not if they are still hard and crunchy at this stage. This is the beginning of cooking your soup. There are a lot of ingredients yet to come, which means the vegetables are going to cook longer.

When do I add the "quick" vegetables?

There is no need to sauté these vegetables in soup. They will overcook if you add them too early. Simply add them to your soup a few minutes before serving.

TIP: If you are making a large quantity of soup, add the "quick" vegetables each time the soup is reheated.

Why do I sauté dried herbs?

Cooking dried herbs is a type of marinating. It rehydrates the plant and draws out both flavor and aroma.

BASIC HERB RULE

☛ **DRIED** herbs and spices: Sauté with the "slow" vegetables.

☛ **FRESH** herbs and spices: Add before serving with the "quick" vegetables.

ॐ

VEGETABLE COOKING CHART (IN MINUTES)

Quick Vegetables (under 10)	Vegetables (10–15)	Slow Vegetables (15–30)
Peppers	Corn	Potatoes
Zucchini	Cauliflower	Turnip
Tender leafy greens: spinach, chard	Green beans	Squash
Garlic*	Mushrooms	Tomatoes
Fresh herbs	Brassica family: broccoli, cabbage, Brussels sprouts	*Brunoises triumvirate: carrots, onion, celery
	Hardy leafy greens: kale, collards	Garlic
	Garlic*	Dried herbs

Garlic can be sautéed at any time.

Remember the *Brunoises Triumvirate*? These three vegetables often cook together, especially in soups and stews. In French cooking, they are often cut in very small dices—called *brunoises*—and then caramelized through sautéing. Think of them as the Three Musketeers of the Soup Kingdom.

GRAINS & BEANS

See Grain and Bean chapters for cooking procedures.

When do I add beans to the soup?

Precook beans and then add them later to soup. Otherwise, all your other ingredients will be overcooked by the time the beans are soft enough to eat.

What about the grains? When do I add them?

Add uncooked grains to soup when sautéing the slow vegetables. Then when you add stock, the grains cook and thicken the soup.

What about leftover cooked grains?

Add leftover or cooked grains with precooked beans and "quick" vegetables. It's fine to use leftover grains; in fact, it's a great way to utilize them. They're already cooked, so they only need to congregate with the rest of the soup.

Can I use any grain in a soup?

Sure. Popular grains are rice and barley. Buckwheat (classified as a fruit) lends a meaty nutty flavor in soups and stews.

THICKENING

There are four basic ways to thicken:

- Grain

- Roux

- Root or Herb

- Puree

Grain

Adding raw grains naturally thickens soup. Grains create a heartier soup that is more nutritious and fulfilling. (See previous section on grains.)

Roux

Roux is commonly used to thicken soup, especially when your soup does not have a lot of grains doing the thickening. Roux is flour and fat. When combined, they create stiff dough. When liquid is added, two things occur: The dough thins out, and the liquid thickens up. Their intersection is a sauce or gravy.

Sounds like how we make Thanksgiving gravy.

You got it. First you remove the bird from the pan. Then you sprinkle in flour, heating and stirring the roux mixture. Next you slowly add water to achieve a desired thickness. Adjust the flavor with salt and pepper, and you're good to gobble! You don't need to start with a roasted turkey in order to make roux. Simply start with fat, add flour, and then liquid.

How much flour for the roux?

It depends on how thick you want your soup.
☛ **MORE FLOUR = THICKER SOUP. LESS FLOUR = THINNER SOUP.**

What kind of flour?

While I prefer to avoid cooking with it, I find that unbleached white flour is the best flour for thickening soups. It is almost pure starch and therefore creates a creamy "sauce" consistency. Whole wheat flour or other flours work well enough, but your soup may possess a gritty texture. Experiment with other flours.

What is the flour/oil ratio?

In general, 2 parts flour to 1 part oil. Basically, you'll use enough flour to absorb the fat.

How much roux do I use?

Like a handful for a pot of soup. If you make too much, you can save it for later.

How do I add the liquid to the roux?

Liquid is added in stages. First, add enough to make a paste-like consistency with the roux (see page 129). Slowly pour this roux sauce into the soup, stirring well to prevent roux lumps.

When do I add roux?

Generally roux is added at the end, to finish the soup. But there is a technique I describe in the next section, where you start the roux at the beginning.

Does the roux have to be a certain temperature?

No. It can be hot or cold. Some chefs have ready-made roux available in their kitchens at all times.

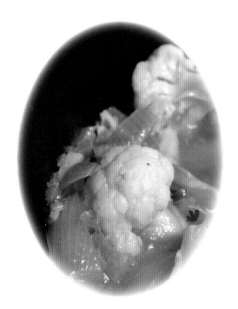

THICKENING SOUP WITH ROUX

Beginning with Roux	Finishing with Roux
→ Heat a pot.	→ Heat a pot.
→ Pour oil into the pot.	→ Pour oil into the pot.
→ Heat the oil.	→ Heat the oil.
→ Sauté main and accessory ingredients.	→ Sauté main and accessory ingredients.
→ Sprinkle flour to create the roux and stir.	→ Add stock and stir.
→ Add stock, a little at a time.	→ Bring to a boil.
→ Add remaining stock.	→ Reduce to a simmer.
→ Bring to a boil.	→ Add roux.
→ Reduce to a simmer.	→ Cook until done.
→ Cook until done.	→ Adjust seasonings.
→ Adjust seasonings.	

Root Starch

Root starches like Kuzu (or *Kudzu*) are traditionally used to thicken Asian soups: Hot and Sour, Wonton, and Egg Drop. Kuzu retains a lovely translucence, whereas roux clouds a soup's appearance. Therefore, Kuzu is more delicate and is useful if you'd like to showcase garnishes in a soup, such as unique vegetables, exotic mushrooms, fresh seafood, or seaweed. Wontons or dumplings also look attractive in soup thickened with Kuzu.

How do I prepare Kuzu?

> → Dissolve Kuzu in enough cold water to make a milky liquid.

> → Add to boiling soup, stirring immediately and swiftly to prevent any clumping.

> → Stir continuously, while boiling, until the Kuzu thickens—about 2–3 minutes.

> → Adjust if necessary, adding more in the same way.

How much Kuzu do I use?

Enough. (Sorry, I couldn't resist.) Use a chunk about the size of a caramel for about a cup of water. That'll thicken a regular pot of soup. But, again . . . use more or less, depending on your preferences (and what you would consider a "regular" pot of soup).

What if I add too much Kuzu?

Thin the soup with more liquid.

No, I mean what if I melt too much Kuzu into the cup before I add it to the soup?

Oh. Then add more liquid to the Kuzu.

What if I don't need all the Kuzu mixture I make?

Store it in the refrigerator. Before reusing, stir well, as it will settle into a big lump.

Why use Kuzu? Why not just use corn starch?

If you don't have Kuzu, use arrowroot. As a last resort, use corn starch. (Sigh. Here I go again.) Corn Starch *is* less expensive, but the nutritional benefits of using Kuzu or arrowroot outweigh their cost. Again folks, we are talking nutrient density here. Arrowroot is less nutritious than Kuzu but more nutritious than corn starch. Corn starch is to thickeners what white flour and sugars are to whole grains. Kuzu is more than nutritious; it is medicinal.

In macrobiotic cooking, Kuzu is touted for its intestinal support in helping to restore beneficial bacteria. It is used as a soothing tea for nausea and stomach ulcers. You'll

NOTE: *Linkgredients* also effectively thicken soups and stews. Add them at the end, to finish your soup.

find Kuzu and arrowroot at any Natural Foods store. I have often sipped Kuzu in hot water after meals, and it does soothe my widdle tummy. It's great for kids' tummies too, because it has no taste and can be added into other drinks.

Puree

Pureeing is a simple, economical way to thicken a soup. When the soup is done cooking, blend it. That's it! By blending, you are also creating a different aesthetic: The soup now resembles a sauce (and, in fact, could be used as a sauce).

How do I puree soup?

My favorite appliance is the . . . wait for it . . . hand-held Immersion blender. I recommend the Cuisinart model ($25.00). Hand-held blenders are fantastic for pureeing soups, sauces, and smoothies. Hand-held blenders are the Chef Henin of appliances. Other blenders include the upright food blender or food processor.

What kinds of soups are pureed?

Purees are typically vegetable soups, such as cream of broccoli, tomato, or mushroom. Fruit soups are also delicious and a great way to utilize summer's bounty. Garnish with raw or cooked pieces of the main ingredient to showcase: shredded beets, chopped carrots, or diced apples. Pureed soups can be hot or cold. Fruit soups tend to be cold.

How much of the soup do I blend?

It depends upon the texture you desire. Basic purees blend a third to half of the soup. Gazpacho is a chunky soup, so you'd want to puree just enough to create a base that holds the ingredients together. Classics like Vichyssoise (cold Potato-Leek soup), Tomato, or Fruit soups blend the entire product.

Not to sound like a broken record . . . but it is up to you. Who says you can't have a chunky Vichyssoise? Who says you can't have a smooth Gazpacho?

Why bring soup to a boil before reducing to a simmer?

This is the most efficient way to cook a soup. Once the water has been brought to a boil, the boil can be maintained on a lower heat, called a *simmer*. If the pot is covered, you need even less heat. This minimizes cooking time and saves energy. Turn the heat down to the point where only a few tiny bubbles pop on the surface of the soup. Keep enough heat for the soup to cook.

TIP: Chill soups before blending to at least room temperature. Hot foods can damage blenders. Or, GET YOURSELF THAT HAND-HELD IMMERSION BLENDER! It can take the heat—no cooling necessary!

While it *is* safer, boiling food also destroys live enzymes, friendly bacteria and cultures, which promote health. Again, you should see just a few bubbles emerge at the surface of the liquid. That way, you maintain the safety zone and continue cooking while salvaging some nutrients.

BASIC SOUP PROCEDURE

MAKING SOUP FROM SCRATCH			
A	**B**	**C**	**D**
"Slow" vegetables Dried herbs & spices Raw grains & *meetz* Liquid: water, stock	Precooked and/or leftover grains, beans, and *meetz*	Roux Kuzu or arrowroot Linkgredients	"Quick" vegetables Fresh herbs & spices

→ Cook A. Bring to a boil and reduce to a simmer.

→ Add B.

→ Add C. Bring to a boil and reduce to a simmer.

→ Add D.

→ Adjust liquid and seasonings to desired taste and consistency.

Dancing, Swinging, Poetry . . . Marinade

Time to get down with marinades. While this is recipe-free cooking, there are basic ratios that work well. For those of you just starting out, you may appreciate the added instruction, but never worry about exact amounts. There is always wiggle room—even in baking—where we need to be the most conscientious about amounts (see Mish Mash).

Marinades are measured in parts or volume, for instance: 2 parts A to 1 part B

- Do you have a CUP? The marinade ratio is 2 CUPS A to 1 CUP B.

- Do you have a BOWL? The marinade ratio is 2 BOWLS A to 1 BOWL B.

- Do you have a GRECIAN . . .

Susie, I get it. I get it.
Good! Now, any questions?

What is the difference between a marinade and a dressing?
It's how you use it. The ingredients are the same, but their application is different. A marinade is used at the beginning or in the preparation stage of a dish. It is used to tenderize or flavor raw product before cooking, as in marinating tempeh or tofu before frying. A dressing is added at the end of preparation, just before serving. You might think of a dressing as something that *dresses* the meal to make it present-able. Marinades are typically spicier, since their flavor is absorbed into raw bland food over time. Dressings are designed to cover and complement food and are added right before eating, so they are generally milder.

☞ For simplicity, I will refer to the following ratios as dressings.

🐦 BASIC DRESSING

TIP: Substitute lemon juice for vinegar.

1 part VINEGAR + 2 parts OIL

Pour vinegar into a container. Add oil. Mix.

That's it! That's dressing. Everything else is accessory.

Traditional dressings typically recommend more oil: 3 to 1, oil to vinegar. For a healthier alternative, I prefer 2 to 1. More oil can always be added. Remember, underseason and adjust versus overseason and regret!

🐦 TRADITIONAL

Basic Dressing + Sweetener + Salt & Pepper

Why add sweetener?

Sweetener mellows the vinegar (or acid) and improves the dressing's flavor.

What kind of sugar?

Avoid white sugar and opt for more nutrient density with honey, rice or maple syrup, Sucanat (dried Cane juice), or other natural sweeteners, like agave. Remember complex carbohydrates? These natural sugars are healthier and tastier.

🐦 TRADITIONAL VARIETIES

TIP: Sweetener is often the secret ingredient when people ask: "What is it about your dressing? I can never duplicate it!"

Garlic = Traditional + Garlic

Garlic may be added to all dressings (except for sweet dressings for fruit salads). It adds delightful flavor. Garlic is my BFF.

How much Garlic?

Add a clove at a time, tasting after each addition. Mince or chop it, finely. Garlic's flavor heightens or blooms with time, so add one clove less than what tastes fine—unless the dressing will be used immediately, in which case use that last clove that might otherwise push the flavor over the edge.

■ **Herbal** = Traditional + Herbs

What kinds of herbs?

Refer to the "Top Ten" listings for a particular flavor. Keep it simple and FARE WELL. When possible, use fresh herbs; they provide vibrant flavor, live enzymes, and water-soluble vitamins. Imagine and experiment. Look through your spice cabinet. What do you have? Parsley and cilantro? Thyme and basil? Sage and dill? Great!

Clove and oregano? Clove and oregano . . . hmmm . . . might be tangy and interesting, but try a small amount first.

The type of herbs may determine the use. If I use Italian herbs, I create Italian dressing. If I use Asian spices, I create Asian dressing, and so on.

■ **Dijon** = Traditional + Mustard

A solid choice is *Grey Poupon* or other quality Dijon mustard. *Nance's Sweet 'n Hot* mustard delivers a zesty kick. Experiment with different mustards; there are hundreds out there.

How much mustard?

I don't know. How much do you like mustard? Add a little. Taste it. Add more if you want more.

■ **Tamari Dressing** = 1 part Tamari + 1 part Vinegar + 2 parts Oil

This is a common, versatile marinade. Make a big batch to have on hand. Substituting tamari for salt adds a richer, tangier flavor.

&❧ CREAMY DRESSINGS

Creamy dressings contain *emulsifiers*—protein substances whose job it is to attract and bond oil to acid, causing the dressing to become creamy or emulsified. They are liquid linkgredients. Emulsifiers are the matchmakers of the Marinade Kingdom.

MAIN EMULSIFIERS:

- Egg

- Tofu

- Nut butters

- Dairy

EGG

Use an egg per cup of dressing.

Okay, not to be difficult here, but you said that we are, like, "above" measuring. Now you're throwing in a cup. What's up?

No, you're right. My bad. But it doesn't have to be *exactly* one cup. Use any basic "cup-type-thingie" in your kitchen: a coffee mug (although most "mugs" are fricken 20 ounces these days . . .) or an empty yogurt container. If you have a measuring cup, fine. Just don't fastidiously measure to the exact cup line. The dressing won't care, and neither should you.

TOFU

2 oz. TOFU = 1 EGG

Use 2 oz. tofu for about a cup of dressing. Substitute tofu for egg in any recipe.

NUT BUTTERS

Use a spoonful of nut butter per cup of dressing. The most popular nut emulsifier is tahini.

DAIRY

Yogurt, sour cream, and buttermilk contribute a marvelous tang to a dressing and luscious creaminess to a salad.

■ Basic Creamy Dressing = Basic or Traditional + Emulsifier

→ Combine all ingredients *except* oil.

→ Let dressing rest for a few minutes.

→ SLOWLY pour in oil while constantly whisking or blending.

→ Adjust flavor.

→ Let dressing rest before serving.

TIP: To further encourage emulsification, add a few drops of water along with the oil.

Why do I let dressing rest?

Remember our Italian Lentil-Barley salad? The dressing, itself, marinates—allowing flavors to mellow and marry. Flavors need time to get to know each other. Be considerate and patient. Hey, it's only a few minutes! This is a good time to clean up a bit.

Why do I SLOWLY add the oil?

First, we pour the oil slowly to let the protein molecules emulsify with the oil and vinegar. Sauces and dressings may separate or "BREAK" if we rush the process and muck the ratio: Too much oil is trying to be emulsified too quickly or with too little vinegar. Picture steroid muscles on small-framed bones; the bones break under too much pressure. When a dressing breaks, it will not be creamy anymore. It looks lumpy—like cottage cheese—oily and separated. Pour the oil slowly while mixing continuously to prevent breakage.

Second, pour oil slowly to control the amount you need. Depending upon personal tastes, one may need more or less than what a "recipe" would call for or even more or less than what tasted good in a previous batch. Pouring slowly prevents the problem of adding too much oil. Remember the *Attack of the 50-foot Tall Dressing*? When you pour slowly, this is less likely to happen.

In what kind of container do I make creamy dressing?

Bowl: Stir well with a fork or whisk.

Bowl with hand-held blender:

> → Add vinegar and egg into bowl.

> → Mix with hand-held blender.

> → Slowly add oil, continuing to blend.

Blender:

> → Place vinegar and egg into blender.

> → Keep blender on *lowest* speed.

> → While blender is *on* with lid *off*, slowly pour in oil as blender mixes the dressing.

Food Processor:

> → *Pulse* vinegar and egg together.

> → Add oil slowly, pulsing the oil into the vinegar mixture.

Once the dressing emulsifies, does it need to re-emulsify?

It should stay put. If it does break, remix (using a blender is preferable to mixing in a bowl). If it remains broken, add some more of the emulsifier and remix.

> NOTE: Broken dressing is edible; it's just not pretty. If you are unable to re-emulsify, go ahead and use it.

■ **Creamy Herb** = Basic Creamy + Herbs

Ever tried *Green Goddess* dressing? This is it. Fresh herbs make an incredible difference in flavor, especially in this dressing. Chop herbs finely.

What herbs do I use?

*Think **GREEN**!* Common herbs are parsley, basil, oregano, thyme, marjoram, and dill. Experiment with different herbs, and again, FARE WELL.

*Think **RED!*** Use red items, like tomato, paprika, red peppers, and heck, even left-over squash.

*Think **BOLD!*** Hot peppers, Tabasco, Worcestershire sauce, garlic, and onion zip it!

■ **Creamy Tamari or Miso** = Basic Creamy + Tamari or Miso

Substituting tamari or miso for salt sweetens the dressing naturally. Miso further thickens the dressing. Both create an Asian flavor that is excellent with pasta, rice, and stir-fry.

■ **Super Healthy Yummy Caesar** = Creamy Tamari or Miso + Garlic + Onion Powder + Nutritional Yeast + Black Pepper

This tastes remarkably like Caesar Dressing but is dairy, egg, and anchovy-free. Use liberally in salads, casseroles, burgers, and roll-ups. Pour on grains for a super-yummy *Rice-a'Roni* flavor.

■ **Creamy French** = Basic Creamy + Mustard

This is the *real* French dressing, not its sugary neon orange American deviation. I earned (yes, not learned, but earned) this recipe from Chef Pierre I would make five gallons at a time (on *purpose*). This authentic version includes *Grey Poupon* and onion or garlic.

■ **Tomato French** = Classic French + Tomato

This is a tangy, more Americanized version of French—similar to store-bought *Catalina* brand dressing.

What kind of tomato?

Hmm . . . let's see what we have, shall we? Bit of ketchup? Some spaghetti sauce? A blob of tomato paste? Or best of all, some chopped tomatoes? How about that "perfectly good" piece of tomato that my mother saved from the family brunch and wrapped in a plastic bag—not the expensive zip-lock kind of bags, but the 200-pack bargain bags with the economical twist ties? (Love you, mommy.) Use what you like, what you got, or whatever "perfectly good" item you could utilize.

■ **Russian** = Tomato French + Chopped Onion, Pickle, and Parsley

Remember grandma's Russian dressing—mayonnaise, catsup, and relish? This new version is much tastier, healthier, and less sugary-sweet. Try it with Sandor Katz's live pickles ("Wild Things" chapter).

ર&.   ર&.   ર&.

Our next section addresses sauces and spreads. Dressings are the natural segue; any dressing can be the base for sauces and spreads.

What's the difference between a dressing and a sauce?
     I'll let you field this one.

 Hey reader! What's the difference between a dressing and a sauce?
     A sauce is . . . thicker than a dressing?

Right. And how do you thicken a sauce?
     Ask me after this next section.

You're getting smarter already.

Sauces and Spreads and Dips: Oh My!

Think of a sauce as a thin spread, and a spread as a thickened sauce. All are creamy or spicy or tangy or sweet and should never overwhelm the food they accompany. Sauces are similar to dressings and marinades in terms of ingredients. The difference is in the amounts of particular ingredients.

Is this confusing? I think I'm making it sound more complicated than it is. Let's take a look at some basic sauce and spread/dip ingredients.

SAUCES AND SPREADS:
THE BASIC RECIPE FORMULA

MAIN & ACCESSORY INGREDIENTS	SAUCE & FLAVORING INGREDIENTS
Beans	Liquid/stock
Nut & seeds	Tomato
Tomato	Lemon
Vegetables: chopped or pureed	Miso
Linkgredients	Tamari
	Nut butters
	Nut milks
	Wine or liqueur (for desserts)
	Herbs & spices

→ Place some of A in a bowl.   → Add some of B.

That's it! Sauces and spreads and dips! Oh, my!

A FEW TIPS:

- Use both raw or cooked ingredients.
- Sauté vegetables and dried spices for richer flavor.
- For optimal flavor, allow the sauce to rest (marinate).

NOTE: Cooked sauces tend to have richer flavor. Raw ingredients tend to have more nutrients. Flavor or nutrition? It's your call.

TIP: Potato is useful when soup or sauce is over-salted. Place 1-2 whole potatoes into the pot and simmer for approximately 30 minutes; lo, they will absorb some of the salt. (Afterward, compost the potatoes.)

THE BASIC BEVERAGES

THE BASIC BEVERAGES

The Good, the Bad, and the Smoothie

I'm easing my way back up on that soapbox, folks. As my pappy says (excruciatingly all too often): *"If I may be so bold . . ."*

People buy too many beverages. Period. Sodas, bottled juices, aseptic packages, etc. create a constant need for aluminum, glass, and plastic containers. These stuff our land-fills, pollute our environment, and waste energy in manufacturing and recycling.

If left alone, our bodies are smart and adaptable.

It's not just a waste of external resources. It's a waste of internal resources. Sodas contain carbonic and phosphoric acids, which can weaken blood vessels and teeth and interfere with the body's pH (acid/alkaline) balance. Most bottled drinks also contain simple sugars, which are acidic. The human body has a normal pH of around 7.4—slightly alka-line. Excessive consumption of acidic products causes the pH to lower and creates an acidic environment within our bodies. This further weak-ens blood vessels, organs, and tissues, raises blood pressure, increases cholesterol, taxes the liver and pancreas, and increases the chances of mothers-in-law moving in permanently.

If left alone, our bodies are smart and adaptable. One way the body attempts to dilute the acidic state is through retaining water. Here the madness ensues. Enter the irony that people drink "diet" sodas as an aid to weight loss. Meanwhile, the body retains water (gains weight) to compensate for the acidity, diluting its environment in an attempt to restore its slightly alkaline state.

. . . people drink "diet" sodas as an aid to weight loss. Meanwhile, the body retains water (gains weight) to compensate for the acidity.

While "internal acidic environments" set the stage for anaerobic-loving diseases like cancer, one should heed the demonic credo. Remember *"Anything worth doing is worth overdoing?"* Remember the laetrile couple? A body in an overly alkaline state is no healthier than an overly-acidic one. It's wonderful that our bodies require a pH of 7.4 because, on a pH scale of 0–14, it establishes such a lovely argument for seeking balance, eh?

What do I drink instead of soda?
Lemon water

Lemon water is quintessential—a refreshing healthful beverage. It is purported to have stimulating properties, which aid in digestion. It also has cleansing properties, which purify the blood, liver, and kidneys, and clear the mind. Drink it often and throughout the day. Slice of lemon in water. Bam.

Apple cider vinegar

Instead of lemon in your water, try RAW UNDISTILLED apple cider vinegar for similar health benefits. Apple cider vinegar contains minerals like potassium, which benefit the heart and regulate cholesterol levels. Both of these beverages can aid in digestion when sipped with and after a meal.

Juices

Choose 100% juice. In Vermont's cool months, we buy freshly pressed apple cider. Winter is the time for fresh-squeezed orange and grapefruit juices. Dilute juice in water to stretch the product. Most juices are overly sweet anyway, so diluting does not detract their flavor.

Create your own sodas!

Mix sparkling water and juice. Add a squirt of citrus for added tang. Use *sparkling spring* water rather than carbonated water or club soda. Sparkling water does not contain carbonic and phosphoric acids.

Fruit smoothies

Smoothies are a wonderful way to honor the Crazybusy. Blend frozen bananas, fruits and fruit juice, yogurt or nut milks. When I can rouse my butt out of bed, I'll make my son a smoothie before he goes to school: yogurt, frozen bananas, maple syrup, berries—whatever's available.

Try *liquados* or *batidos*—blended fresh fruit with water or milk. These are streamlined smoothies. Use equal amounts fruit or vegetable and dilute with spring water or milk. Of course you will use that hand-held blender that you now love so much. Aren't you glad you bought it?

NOTE: The ratio of son hugs to smoothies is 1 HUG to 1 SMOOTHIE.

Fresh juice

Fresh-squeezed juices are more work, but may save money in the long run. They skyrocket nutritional density. Juices may be made from most fruits, vegetables, and herbs and are often combined for optimal benefits: carrot and ginger, beets and parsley, berries and pineapples, etc.

How do I make fresh juice?

You need a juicer; this is the investment part. I recommend the Champion or the Juiceman; both have exceptional quality and value.

First you got me cooking, and then I'm grinding my own flour. Now I'm juicing? Susie, do you have a job?

Seriously, I get it. Juicing is a pain in the neck: time consuming, messy, and you know . . . rampantly challenges our crazybusy culture. But if you are serious about maintaining health or extracting optimal energy benefits from your food . . . if you want to get paid the most for your job . . . it's worth it.

I would be negligent if I didn't inform you of these nutrient-dense options. They are not listed to make you feel guilty or remind you of how you don't care about your health. You may not always choose the healthiest foods. None of us do! But it is helpful to know what they are, so that you can decide for yourself.

If you're curious about fresh juices, don't run out and buy a juicer. Remember the under-season maxim. Try fresh juice at Natural Foods stores first, to see if you enjoy the flavor and notice the health benefits. Many stores have smoothie and juice bars. Squeeze some fresh grapefruit juice or smush papaya in a glass with a shot of milk. Embrace good health, brick by brick . . . one meal at a time.

Remember to smile! You're taking care of yourself!

Embrace good health, brick by
brick . . . one meal at a time.

Coffee, Tea, or Me?

So you like the jolt from caffeinated drinks? Well, while I am still up here on the soapbox . . .

THE ASSAULT OF THE JOLT

Let us review our body's fuel system. Whole food is made up of complex carbohydrates. "Complex" describes long chains of sugar or starch molecules. These long chains could be compared to big logs. Our body is the wood stove. The body stores these "big logs"—complex chains—in our muscles, like a woodpile. In order to keep the fire burning at a steady pace, the body needs shorter chains or smaller pieces of wood. The body must convert long chains into shorter or "simple" chains—chop up big logs into stove-length pieces. These simple sugar chains are released into the bloodstream and distributed throughout the body wherever energy is needed—just as logs burn in the woodstove and distribute heat throughout the house. The body is capable of burning only a few simple chains at a time. It takes 2–4 hours to burn a big log in the fire. Therefore, long chains provide a long steady supply of energy. People typically eat 3–5 times a day, because that is how many times they need to stoke their fires.

. . . people typically eat 3–5 times a day, because that is how many times they need to stoke their fires.

Processed, refined food is primarily simple carbohydrates. "Simple" describes short chains of molecules of sugar and starches. These short chains might be compared to easy-burning fuel: kindling, paper, or even lighter fluid. Sure, they burn easily and readily, supplying a familiar "burst" of energy. But they also burn *quickly*. Imagine keeping a bonfire going with only paper and lighter fluid. You'd be standing over the fire all night, pouring the stuff directly onto the fire. You can't store simple sugars. Or rather, you don't store them as readily burnable fuel, like complex chains are stored. Simple chains are stored as fat.

Think of fat as a big stump: It is easier to convert a piece of split firewood (complex carbohydrate) into energy than a big stump (fat). You don't start a fire with a stump; you toss one on after the bonfire is blazing. Once simple sugars are stored as fat, the only way to burn them off is through blazing—sustained aerobic exercise. If you plan on eating fat, you better have a big, efficient hot stove (high metabolism) in order to burn it.

Determining if stress is good or bad ultimately depends upon your perception of the events unfolding and your reaction to them.

Most foods contain sugars and starches. Sugars are used quickly by the body, absorbed from the blood into the cells. Starches are stored first and then converted to sugar as needed. Complex or long-chained sugars are also stored in the body until use. The frequency and amount of conversion depends upon one's metabolism. Your metabolism depends upon your lifestyle. For instance, if you have an active lifestyle or experience positive stress (eustress), you will burn up your sugars and starches more rapidly (and effectively) than if you are sedentary, unfit, and experience negative stress (*distress*) in your life.

I thought stress was bad?

Actually, no, it's not. It is predominant in all of our lives. *Stress* is a concept that refers to a change in the mind, body, or spirit, due to an experience or *stressor*. The "experience" can be "bad," such as a car crash. It can be "good," such as winning the lottery. On the other hand, the car crash might result in a new car. Winning the lottery may turn into one of the worst events of your life. Thus, determining if stress is good or bad ultimately depends upon your *perception* of the events unfolding and your *reaction* to them. This, in turn, affects how your body responds to that stressor.

It can get even more complicated. Let's say you are planning a wedding. You might consider this *eustress* while your partner might consider it *distress*. Some people thrive in chaos and last-minute deadlines, while other people thrive in routine and discipline. Stress is definitely in the eye of the beholder, and it does affect how we burn our bodies' fuel.

To quote my favorite author, Max Shulman, "but I digress."

The liver converts all carbohydrates into glucose. Glucose is our body's burnable energy source. Complex carbohydrates are first stored as glycogen in the liver and muscles to be converted into glucose as needed. As our glucose levels deplete, our fire begins to go out, and so we add more logs to the fire.

SUGAR	>>>	GLUCOSE	>>>	ENERGY			
STARCH	>>>	GLYCOGEN	>>>	GLUCOSE	>>>	ENERGY	

As sugar is utilized as energy—as we burn our logs—the adrenal glands and pancreas sense a drop in glucose levels. When the drop is significant enough, the pancreas releases *glucagon*—a hormonal secretion—into the blood. Glucagon cues the liver to convert glycogen into glucose, and the blood sugar safely returns to normal levels.

We can either get logs from our muscles (glycogen) or from new food (glucose). If we don't have enough glycogen stored, we become hungry and consume more glucose. If we eat too much, we must store some of that glucose as glycogen.

The pancreas is the nagging housewife, and glucagon is her nag. The liver is the nagged husband who has to go out into the cold and get more firewood to stoke the fire. As we deplete our glycogen storage (burn our logs), we experience hunger (the house gets cold), and the nagging cycle continues.

Enter caffeine. Caffeine is an aggressive stimulant; it overstimulates the adrenal glands and bullies the pancreas into releasing glucagon, which causes a flood of sugar—whether or not it is needed. This high level of blood sugar stimulates the release of an opposing hormone, *insulin*, which is the glucose watchdog. Insulin is like the Secret Service; it whisks glucose quickly out of the bloodstream, so we don't suffer from acidosis. Once again, blood sugar lowers, signaling the pancreas to release more glucagon, which once again cues the liver to begin converting glycogen to glucose, dumping more sugar into the bloodstream. The "jolt" we feel from caffeine comes primarily from excess sugar in the blood—sugar that was meant to be stored and released slowly over time, sustaining us steadily for many hours. The more caffeine we drink, the more the madness ensues. Think of caffeine as a convincing friend who loves to party. This friend convinces you to go to the ATM and withdraw 500 bucks. You blow a weeks' wages in one night. Drinking coffee initiates a party in your bloodstream.

The way we burn our sugar affects our behaviors. We either have "sustainable" personalities or "rave party" personalities.

What's so bad about a sugar party? It sounds fun.
Well, play it out. Think of sugar as money. Sugar in the bloodstream is money in your pocket. Stored sugar is money in the bank. Burning sugar too quickly is like spending money too quickly. When you use up your sugar, you've withdrawn all your funds. Now you got no more money. That money in the bank was meant to pay for bills throughout the week rather than drop a wad of cash for an instant rave party in your bloodstream.

Imagine a bonfire in your backyard. Sure, for an hour you're nice and toasty, with a roaring fire blazing. After that, you're freezing and your woodpile has been squandered.

I'll go one further; I believe that the way we burn our sugar affects our behaviors. We either have "sustainable" personalities or "rave party" personalities.

When people say they cannot function without coffee, they are correct.

The more caffeine one drinks, the more the body begins to rely upon it to initiate glucagon and insulin release. It's like the kid who becomes dependent upon antibiotics to stimulate his immune system. When people say they cannot function without coffee, they are correct.

Fortunately, the body is smart and adaptable. This dependence is reversible for most people. But when the wood stove breaks, malfunctioning such as diabetes, hypoglycemia, and Addison's disease develops. Some health practitioners assert a correlation between compromised fuel systems with cancer and autoimmune diseases. At the very least, you are continually exhausted and unable to regulate your energy. And if you want to maintain a crazybusy lifestyle, you better have a properly functioning furnace.

What other foods contain caffeine?

Chocolate contains caffeine. So do some herbs: tea, maté, Kola nut, and guarana, to name a few. Oddly, cigarettes contain caffeine. Some medicines contain it, like the *Excedrin* brand of aspirin.

Sounds like caffeine and white sugar will make me crazy and fat.

Yep. And there are more problems. You may be destroying yourself—literally.

Let me explain.

First, by depleting your stored glycogen, you are constantly hungry. Caffeine will continue stressing your adrenal glands and pancreas, forcing your liver to use up your glucose. Constant consumption also signals the release of stress hormones such as cortisol and adrenaline. These chemicals cause riots in your system. The body is tricked into feeling "energized" when, in fact, it is experiencing a stress response—same as a *fight or flight* response. Basically, your body is under attack, inundated with chemical warfare. Exciting, sure; but balanced? Nuh uh.

Another problem occurs when people eat simple sugars with their caffeine (coffee

If you want to maintain a crazybusy lifestyle, you

better have a properly functioning furnace.

and a donut). Excessive simple sugars are dumped into the bloodstream. Insulin whisks the excessive sugar out of the bloodstream (stored as fat) and causes a quick drop in blood sugar. Meanwhile, the caffeine is forcing the liver to unnecessarily convert previously stored sugar, which soon depletes the glycogen supply. You've just burned all your stored sugar and replaced it with a bunch of stored fat. It's a triple whammy. Ba-ba-*BOOM!*

Here's where it gets weird. Let's say you want to keep the party going, but you got no funds. What do you do? You might borrow some money. Or if you are truly desperate, you might resort to stealing.

Your body thinks in the same way. It must receive sugar from *somewhere.* If it's not getting it from outside sources (food) and internal sources (stored glycogen), where do you think it gets it?

From fat?

You would think so. But, no, not normally. Fat is the least efficient energy source to burn. We burn sugar, starch, and even protein before fat. Unless we have high metabolisms, we store most of the fat we eat. Most of us die with most of our fat.

So, I ask you again. Where do you think the body derives its energy supply?

From . . . the rest of the body?

Bingo. The liver initiates self-cannibalism and begins tearing down the house: converting the body's muscle and tissue into usable sugar so that the body can survive! We'll burn any wood and paper product in the house and then start tearing down the walls, posts, and floors. If we're freezing to death, we'll burn whatever we got.

Yikes!

Tell me about it. And it gets worse.

Worse than self-cannibalism?

Hear me out. We're talking about burning sugar, right? Let me back up a bit. In "Amazing Grains and Simple Sugars," I discussed the value of consuming whole grains in one's diet:

Nature knew exactly what she was doing when she created the whole grain. Whole grains contain all the nutrients necessary to properly assimilate that particular grain's carbohydrate. In fact, all the nutrients contained in any whole food are those nutrients needed to properly assimilate that particular whole food. Nature has researched all the chemistry for us; we simply eat her intricate science.

Sugars and starches are carbohydrates. Carbohydrates are *macronutrients*—nutrients that the body needs in *macro* (large) amounts. Proteins and fats are also macronutrients. *Micronutrients* are nutrients that the body needs in smaller amounts, such as vitamins, minerals, and enzymes.

Carbohydrates, like any macronutrient, need micronutrients in order to be assimilated. Without these micronutrients, carbohydrates cannot be burned and are stored as fat—

We have an over-abundance of food production and an epidemic of obesity, while citizens suffer from malnutrition.

or worse. Excessive protein, for instance, can become toxic in the body by creating a buildup of uric acid, which exacerbates inflammatory diseases like arthritis and gout. When you eat white sugar or starch and the meal does not supply ample micronutrients, then **your body is forced to extract those micronutrients from its own muscles and tissues**. More autocannibalism occurs in an attempt to utilize this excess sugar dumped into your blood. It's either autocannibalism or death by acidosis. Bodies tend to choose death as a last resort. If someone held a gun up to your head and said, "Death or diabetes. You choose." What are you gonna choose? Exactly. So does your body.

If we do not supply the necessary micronutrients every time we ingest caffeine or white sugar, we continue to "borrow" them. And to further complicate this, many vitamins (B & C) are watersoluble, meaning un-storable. Whatever we don't use immediately is flushed out of the system (that's the bright-yellow smelly pee we have, after taking a B-complex supplement).

We see how well this strategy works for our nation's economic system. Self-cannibalism is our attempt to reconcile our physiological debt. This is one cause of malnutrition in first-world countries. Here in America, we have an overabundance of food production and an epidemic of obesity, while citizens suffer from malnutrition and nutrient-deprived illnesses. This crazybusy consumption also accounts for the phenomenal irony of the anorexic physique: severely underweight people consume their own muscle and tissue

Severely underweight people consume their
own muscle and tissue in order to survive,
while unburnable fat remains hoarded.

in order to survive, while unburnable fat remains hoarded. Malnutrition is not caste dependent; it is diet dependent. The typical American diet consists heavily of simple sugars and processed foods, which are mainly empty calories.

What's an empty calorie?

An empty calorie is the opposite of nutrient density. A calorie is a food unit of energy, and "empty" implies that it contains little to no nutrients along with that supplied energy. White sugar is an example of an empty calorie food.

In a diet rich in empty calories, whatever micronutrients we *do* eat are first spent on dealing with these empty calories—excess sugars—instead of serving their primary purposes—physiological functions like regulating body systems, rebuilding cells, stimulating the immune system, etc.

Tsk, tsk, tsk. What a waste of precious resources.

Speaking of empty calories, let us return to hydrogenated plastics, aka "fats." Hydrogenated oils have been used in nutritional research to induce essential fatty acid *deficiencies* in both animal and human volunteers. Think about it: This product is used *specifically* and *intentionally* to create a nutritional deficiency. Let's dumb that down. This product takes nutrients from your body. It steals money from your nutritional bank account. Hydrogenated fats go one step beyond empty calorie: They are *negative* calories. And we are paying good money to be robbed.

What are alternatives to white sugar? How about high fructose corn syrup?

Good God, don't get me started. High Fructose Corn Syrup (HFCS) is a simple sugar, so it does all those nasty things, plus it does something weird; it slips the body a rufie during the rave party. HFCS inebriates the hypothalamus—the part of the brain responsible for signaling fullness. HFCS delays the hypothalamus' satiation signal, encouraging you to overeat. You just don't know that you're full! This brings in more simple sugar that gets dumped in the system too quickly, keeping the party going and the need to borrow even more nutrients.

What sugar substitute would you recommend?

Overall, I would recommend the natural sugars, like honey, maple or rice syrup, and agave nectar. But if you are looking for a sugar substitute, I would recommend Stevia—hands down. Stevia is an herb that has been sold in Natural Foods markets for years. It has recently taken a popular shift into mainstream markets. Stevia, while intensely sweet, is also consumed for its beneficial balancing properties. Stevia has been reported to assist in regulating blood glucose levels and has been recommended by some alternative health practitioners as an aid in diabetes and hypoglycemia.

Stevia is a sugar substitute and a blood sugar-regulating nutrient, both in one. How many sugar substitutes can you say *that* about? Speaking of substitutes . . .

☞ STAY AWAY FROM ASPARTAME AND ARTIFICIAL SUGARS!

Malnutrition is not caste-dependent; it is diet-dependent.

Aspartame—or NutraSweet—is trouble. Aspartame is composed of two main substances: *methanol* and a synthetic version of the amino acid *phenylalanine.* Phenylalanine is known as a "brain protein," coordinating brain function in a process similar to insulin regulating blood sugar levels. The synthetic phenylalanine in aspartame is its evil twin. It overexcites the brain, causing erratic thoughts and behaviors. Methanol is wood alcohol—toxic in the body and harmful to the liver. In many documented studies spanning decades, aspartame has been linked to various neuropsychiatric disorders, including panic attacks, mood changes, visual hallucinations, manic episodes, and isolated dizziness. Aspartame has been linked to brain diseases such as migraines, tumors, Parkinson's, seizures, mental illness, and autoimmune diseases, such as lupus and shingles.

Acesulfame K is no better. This creep stimulates insulin secretion, which overworks the body's sugar regulating system. It's like a boss who micromanages you, causing performance anxiety and an unproductive work environment. It has been shown to instigate and aggravate hypoglycemia.

Acesulfame K has been linked to many kinds of tumors. In several rodent studies, even when less than maximum doses were given, tumors manifested everywhere: brain tumors, breast tumors, lung tumors, several forms of leukemia, rare types of tumors of other organs (such as the thymus gland), and chronic respiratory disease.

Since its hasty FDA approval in 1988, the safety of acesulfame K has come into question. Aspartame's GRAS (Generally Regarded as Safe) status has also been petitioned several times and each petition has been overturned or abandoned. The market for these products has been too strong to warrant repeals.

Remember mom's Tab? It contained good ol' saccharin. In a word: cancer.

We no longer see saccharin on the market, because a few decades of protestation and boycott finally shifted mindsets. But aspartame and acesulfame K—and more artificial sweeteners to come—are still in the transitional stages of being concurrently challenged and distributed.
Take a proactive step. Defend your health with healthy options. If you do want to avoid sugar, use Stevia. Stevia is sweet and, amazingly, doesn't cause cancer. And it is catching on. Now that is it popular enough for "them" to make a profit, you can easily find it in mainstream markets.

Would you ever advocate for white sugar?

Well, it's better to eat white sugar than a synthetic sweetener (other than Stevia). At least white sugar is an actual food product, although people eat so much of it that it acts more like a poison or drug than food in their body, creating manic highs and depressive lows, dangerously acidic pH levels, and cannibalistic survival methods.

What do you recommend I drink?

Drink herbal teas instead of coffee, caffeinated teas, or sodas. Herbs are more nutritious than most foods and have little to no calories. Peppermint and chamomile teas are excellent replacements for caffeine drinks. There are hundreds of herbs to choose from; check out the selection at your Natural Foods stores or supermarkets. As with anything, if you choose to drink caffeinated beverages, do it in moderation. 1-2 servings a day is reasonable.

The healthiest way to prevent all these issues is with proper diet. Eat a variety of whole foods to cover all nutritional requirements. You do not experience a "high" when eating wholesome food, nor do you experience a "low." You experience a plateau—steady and serene.

An interesting problem with good health or balance is that it is invisible. Distress or imbalance is *noticeable*. A healthy state is calm and subtle. Health is the absence of feeling "something" all the time. We need to feel *grateful* for this absence of "something." Eventually what you'll feel is peace. Never take it for granted.

The Non-Milk of Human Kindness

Dairy products are excellent sources of protein. They also earn props in providing calcium, vitamins D and B12, and Folic acid—all elusive in vegetarian diets. But many people are allergic or have intolerance to dairy. Dairy's sugars and proteins can cause digestive revolts. The revolt may begin with the act of heating dairy. Heating or *pasteurizing* dairy products does kill potentially *harmful* bacteria, but it also destroys *beneficial* bacteria and enzymes that facilitate the digestive process. Consuming cultured or raw milk may remedy lactose intolerance. Cultured foods, in general, are better tolerated due to their abundance of beneficial bacteria and enzymes. Yogurt, kefir, and cheese are cultured dairy products. Raw milk and milk products are found at local farms. Check your local food co-op or farmer's market for sources.

When omitting dairy from your diet, you can still derive calcium, vitamin D, and other animal-based nutrients with a little effort: Alternative milks save the day. And they are taking the market by storm. Non-milks are fantastic in cereals, baking, sauces, milkshakes, or by the glass. They look and taste quite like cow milk and have a lovely sweet flavor. They come flavored and plain, with or without added nutrients. Some of my favorite nut milks include hazelnut, almond, and coconut. Pacific Foods puts out terrific products.

Soy milk is now so common that it is comparable to cow milk in availability and price. Soy milk comes in several flavors: original, vanilla, chocolate, and carob (similar to chocolate but without the caffeine or sugar). Soybeans contain a complete protein—like animal protein—and are rich in calcium and phosphorus, just like "regular" milk (moo).

Rice milk is another delicious alternative. Rice milk and its fermented cousin, *Amazake* (fermented rice milk—a sweeter version), are both rich and creamy. They are loaded with complex carbohydrates and B vitamins. Go, nutrient density!

Nut milks are pretty easy to make:

TIP: Water-to-nut ratio is 3-to-1.

→ Soak nuts overnight.

→ The next day, drain off water, and add fresh water.

→ Blend nuts and water well. Strain.

→ Add salt, vanilla, carob, or sweetener, if desired.

→ Chill before using.

BEYOND THE BASICS

BEYOND
THE BASICS

Mish Mash

In the blissful, imaginative, dancing, swinging, poetry reciting, rule-free world of recipe-free cooking, baking is definitely the exception. Food does not change much in cooking, chemically speaking: Raw food softens, soups thicken, flavors bloom. In the world of cooking, if you plant a turnip, you get a turnip; it's just a better tasting, easier to digest turnip. In the land of baking, however, ingredients blend together to form something completely different! Flour, sugar, eggs, and oil become mousse, cake, cookies, and pie. Gluten activates. Sugars caramelize. Albumin coagulates. Salts and liquids cause batters to rise and bubble. Shapes, textures, and colors transform dramatically.

Remember Mish Mash? The game my best friend, Arla, and I played after school?

One time, we were making banana bread, and I forgot to add the baking powder. Panicking, we pulled the loaf pan out of the oven. We stirred in a spoonful of baking powder into the hot baking batter and then returned it to the oven. That might've been my first physics lesson in culinary arts: Timing is everything. Next was my first chemistry lesson. The bread did not rise. All we did was add lumps and crevices to the unrisen bread.

For years I have tried, unsuccessfully, to Mish Mash in baking. So sue me; I'm stubborn. I'm a "Stew Gal," preferring to toss ingredients into a bowl, stir them together, drizzle with intuition, and create fine soups and salads. But when I apply this to desserts, I create the same flat, rubbery pancake-pudding-cookie patties every time. It's amazing! I have been Mish Mashing since I was in diapers and still cannot bake without a recipe.

However, with this being a recipe-free cookbook and my being stubborn, how about a compromise? The following "recipes" are offered as guidelines to gain an understanding about baking procedures. These recipes will work, but remember to observe and retain, modifying wet and dry ingredients as necessary. For more exact or specific ingredients and amounts, do consult a recipe. Otherwise, have fun with your own version of Mish Mash.

BAKE FOOD UNTIL IT'S DONE

Use your senses! Baked goods will:

SIGHT: *appear* **done**
- lightly browned, slightly rounded and risen
- firm not jiggling when shaken
- fruit bubbles will pop on the surface

TOUCH: *feel* **done**
- a knife or toothpick comes out clean when inserted
- the top springs back when lightly pressed down

HEARING: *sound* **done**
- a slight sizzle or poofing sound of air escapes from warm bubbles on the surface
- bubbles rumble on custard surfaces

SMELL: *smell* **done**
- a delicious aroma will fill the kitchen
- food will smell "browned" or "toasty"

TASTE: *taste* **done**
- well, you know . . .

NOTE: Baked goods need to cool before eating. Let them rest for at least 15 minutes.

TIP: All baked goods will continue to cook after being removed from the oven. This is called "carry-over cooking." To reduce carry-over cooking, cool baked goods on a rack and remove them from their pans after a few minutes. Underbake goods slightly, to ensure moistness—especially cookies and brownies.

BASIC BAKING TIPS

OVEN TEMPERATURES	MEASUREMENTS
HOT: 450°F	SMALL SPOON = TEASPOON
MEDIUM: 350°F	BIG SPOON = TABLESPOON
LOW: 300°F	

BASIC BAKING INGREDIENTS:

- FLOUR: wheat or barley are most common, but experiment with other flours
- FAT: butter, lard, or oil
- EGG: 1 medium egg = 2 oz. tofu
- SWEETENER: honey, molasses, maple syrup, rice syrup, Sucanat, raw sugar (use seldom), mixed fruit concentrate, apple juice
- LIQUID: milk, soy or rice milk, *Amazake,* nut milk, apple juice, yogurt, buttermilk, or water
- FLAVORING: vanilla, flavored liqueurs, spices, fruit juices, citrus rinds, coconut, etc.
- FRUIT OR VEGETABLE: grated apple, banana, carrot, zucchini, mashed pumpkin or squash
- GARNISH: nuts, seeds, dried fruits, cranberries, fresh berries, poppy seeds
- BAKING "AGENTS": baking powder, baking soda, Cream of Tartar

A recipe contains **WET INGREDIENTS:**	A recipe also contains **DRY INGREDIENTS:**
Fats	Flours
Liquid sweeteners	Grains
Liquids	Granulated sweeteners
Fresh fruits and purees	Spices
	Nuts & seeds
	Dried fruit
	Baking agents

BASIC BAKING PROCEDURES

There are three basic baking procedures:

1. **WET INTO DRY**

2. **SHORT DOUGH**

2. **SWEET SAUCE**

1. WET INTO DRY

This is the standard baking procedure for most baking recipes:

→ Mix DRY ingredients in a bowl.

→ Mix WET ingredients in another bowl.

→ Add the WET into the DRY. Mix until *just* combined.

→ Pour into greased and floured pan or scoop onto baking sheets.

→ Bake until *just* done.

→ Remove from oven and allow carry-over cooking for a few minutes.

→ Remove from pan or baking sheets and transfer to a cooling rack.

TIP: In WET INTO DRY, all ingredients should be room temperature.

Why mix until "just combined"?

Most flours contain gluten. When liquid is added to flour, gluten is activated. Gluten contains a network of elastic strands, which form the structure of bread. Gluten develops: through mixing, kneading, and then resting. The more dough is handled, the more the gluten develops. While this is essential for bread making, it is certain death to pastries; they are intended to be light and fluffy.

Both wet and dry ingredients also need to be combined separately *before* being combined together. Not only does this minimize the gluten development, but combining wet ingredients also creates air, which helps the dessert to rise. The more we stir wet ingredients, the lighter and fluffier that dessert will be. Mixing separately also ensures that ingredients are mixed appropriately (versus finding bits of random egg white or a lump of flour popping up in your bread). With both wet and dry nicely prepared, *then* we combine them together.

2. SHORT DOUGH

Short Dough method is used for pies, tarts, and delicate pastry shells. Short Dough method differs from Wet into Dry, not in ingredients but in procedure. **Short Dough has one extra step: Combine DRY ingredients, *then add fat*, and then add WET ingredients.**

→ Mix DRY ingredients together in a bowl.

→ Mix WET ingredients together in a separate bowl.

→ Add fat to the DRY ingredients:

- Cut fat into small pieces.

- "Cut-in" to DRY ingredients: Squeeze the fat into the flour with your fingers with a pressing or rubbing motion.

→ When the mixture resembles corn meal, add WET ingredients:

- Sprinkle the ingredients around the bowl.

- Lift and stir with a fork.

- Stir until *just* combined.

- Shape into a ball.

→ Chill the dough before using, to relax the gluten.

The secret to successful short dough is . . . COLD and FAST! Keep flour and butter refrigerated and water **icecold**. Each ingredient needs to be cold in order to prevent the gluten from developing. Ingredients need to be combined quickly for flaky, crumbly pastry.

3. SWEET SAUCE

Sweet sauce is made from liquid, sweetener, and thickener. The final product is determined by how thick the sauce is. Thin sauce is *Crème Anglaise*—used as a sauce for cakes and a base for ice cream. Thickened *Crème Anglaise* is pudding or custard, and thickened custard is *flan* or pie filling.

→ Mix the thickener: Beat eggs, dissolve Kuzu, or whip tofu, and set aside.

→ Heat liquid and sweetener, bringing *just* to a boil.

→ Remove from heat and add some liquid into the thickener while whipping quickly.

→ Pour this mixture into the rest of the liquid, whipping quickly.

→ Return to stove on medium heat. Whisk vigorously to prevent lumps.

→ Continue to stir slowly and continuously, until the sauce thickens.

→ Remove from heat, stir a few more times, and transfer into a container.

→ Glaze the top with fat OR cover with plastic wrap to prevent skin from forming.

→ Chill until cold OR use as is for pie filling.

WET INTO DRY METHOD

CAKE

MEDIUM OVEN for 20–30 minutes

1 cup sweetener	pinch of salt
1 cup fat	flavoring
2 eggs	optional garnish: 1 cup fruit,
1 cup liquid	vegetable, or grain
2 cups flour	
1 small spoon baking powder	

→ WET INTO DRY method.

→ Mix WET ingredients *well.* Then add DRY.

QUICK BREAD or MUFFIN

MEDIUM OVEN for 20–45 minutes

1 cup sweetener	1 small spoon baking soda
½ cup fat	pinch of salt
1 egg	flavoring
½ cup liquid	optional garnish: 1 cup fruit,
2 cups flour	vegetable, or grain

→ WET INTO DRY method.

→ Mix WET into DRY ingredients until *just combined.*

COOKIE

MEDIUM OVEN for 5–15 minutes

1 cup sweetener	1 small spoon baking soda
½ cup fat	pinch of salt
2 eggs	flavorings
1 cup flour	optional garnish: 1 cup of fruit
1 cup rolled grain flakes	and/or nuts

→ WET INTO DRY method.

→ Mix WET ingredients *well.* Then add DRY.

→ Spoon onto greased cookie sheet—press down and shape.

→ Bake until *ALMOST* done.

BROWNIE

MEDIUM OVEN for 20 minutes

1 cup sweetener

½ cup fat

2 eggs

2 cups flour

1 small spoon baking soda

¼ cup carob powder or chocolate product

optional garnish: 1 cup of chocolate chips or nuts

→ WET INTO DRY method.

→ Follow COOKIE procedure.

MOLASSES COOKIE or GINGERBREAD

Cookie: MEDIUM OVEN for 5–15 minutes

Gingerbread: MEDIUM OVEN for 45 minutes

1 cup unsulphured molasses

½ cup fat

1 egg

½ cup boiling water

2 cups flour

1 small spoon baking soda

pinch of salt

flavoring: fresh or powdered ginger

→ WET INTO DRY method.

→ Follow COOKIE or CAKE procedure.

→ Stir in boiling water LAST.

→ Allow batter to settle a few minutes before baking.

PANCAKE

MEDIUM-HIGH HEAT for 5 minutes

2 big spoons sweetener	2 small spoons baking powder
2 big spoons oil	flavorings
1 egg	optional garnish: 1 cup of fruit,
1 cup milk	nuts, or chocolate chips
1 cup flour	

→ WET INTO DRY method.

→ Mix WET into DRY until *just combined.*

→ Spoon batter onto greased skillet.

→ Cook on one side until there are several bubbles on the surface. Then flip the cake.

→ Cook until the pancake begins to steam.

→ Check the first pancake: Cut it open to assure proper cooking.

❧ SHORT DOUGH METHOD

PIE CRUST

MEDIUM OVEN for 10 minutes

Makes 2 crusts

2 cups flour	water
1/2 cup fat	small pinch of salt

→ SHORT DOUGH method.

→ For cream pies, precook the crust.

→ For fruit pies, use a raw (uncooked) crust.

TART DOUGH

MEDIUM OVEN for 10 minutes

Makes 2 crusts

crust	1 big spoon
1 egg	sweetener

→ SHORT DOUGH method.

→ Precook crust, before adding filling.

BISCUIT

MEDIUM OVEN for 10 minutes

2 big spoons sweetener

½ cup butter

½ cup milk

2 cups flour

1 small spoon baking powder

pinch of salt

→ SHORT DOUGH method.

→ Scoop dough onto floured surface.

→ Roll or press to 1-inch thickness.

→ Cut into circles or squares.

→ Bake until done.

🐚 SWEET SAUCE METHOD

BASIC SWEET SAUCE—PUDDING or CUSTARD

1/2 cup sweetener	2 cups milk
4 egg yolks or 3 big spoons Kuzu	flavorings

→ SWEET SAUCE method.

→ Adjust egg (or Kuzu) amounts for desired thickness.

CHIFFON PIE or MOUSSE

Basic Sweet Sauce	optional garnish: coconut,
1 cup whipped cream	chocolate, fruit, or nuts

→ SWEET SAUCE method.

→ Fold whipped cream into sauce.

→ For pie: Pour into precooked pie shell

→ For mousse: Pour into individual glasses.

→ Chill several hours.

PUMPKIN PIE

MEDIUM OVEN for 45 minutes

Basic Sweet Sauce

2 cups mashed pumpkin

→ SWEET SAUCE method

→ Pour into uncooked pie shell.

CHEESECAKE

MEDIUM OVEN for 60 minutes

Crust:

2 cups graham cracker crumbs

½ stick of butter, softened or melted

→ Mix together.

→ Press into bottom and sides of a pan.

Filling:

1 cup sweetener   flavoring: vanilla, orange or lemon

4 eggs   rind, flavored liqueurs

4–8 oz. packages cream cheese

→ Blend filling *well.*

→ Bake until done.

→ Chill THOROUGHLY before eating. Overnight is best.

❧ OTHER BAKING METHODS

BASIC YEASTED BREAD

HOT *AND* MEDIUM OVEN for 40–60 minutes

2 ½ cups warm liquid	1 small spoon salt
1 big spoon yeast	7 cups flour

Optional:

1 big spoon fat	1 big spoon sweetener

→ Stir water, yeast, and sweetener together until dissolved.

→ Add some flour and stir. Let the batter rest a few minutes.

→ Add the remaining flour and salt. Stir until firm, and then knead
    dough for 10 minutes.

→ Shape into a ball. Let rise in warm area until dough doubles in size—
    about 1–2 hours.

→ Punch the dough to remove the air, knead a couple times, and shape into a
    round loaf or place in a greased loaf pan.

→ Let rise a second time. The second rising takes about half the time.

→ When dough doubles its size, bake in a HOT OVEN for 15 minutes.

→ Reduce heat to a MEDIUM OVEN.

→ Bake until done: Tap the bottom of the loaf. It will sound hollow, like a drum.

→ Remove from oven and pan.

→ Allow bread to cool before eating.

CRISP

MEDIUM OVEN for 30 minutes

Crisp topping:

½ cup sweetener

1 big spoon fat

2 cups rolled oats or barley

flavoring

Make enough topping to cover your fruit base.

Fruit base:

4 cups fruit	1 big spoon Kuzu or starch
2 big spoons sweetener	flavoring

→ Cut fruit into small pieces (leave small fruit, like berries, whole).

→ Toss in Kuzu and sweetener. Adjust sweetening to taste.

→ Place in baking pan and cover with crisp topping.

→ Bake until done.

GRANOLA

MEDIUM OVEN for 30 minutes

Basic Crisp

garnish: dried fruits and nuts

→ Combine ingredients.

→ Spread on greased flat cookie sheet.

→ Bake, stirring every ten minutes, until done.

→ Cool and store in glass jars.

GELATIN

Gelatin is made from fruit juice and gelatin. Healthy versions of gelatin include Kuzu, arrowroot, or *Kanten* (aka Agar Agar) flakes—a type of seaweed.

Ratio: 1 cup juice to 1 big spoon gelatin.

→ Dissolve flakes in a little water or juice.

→ Bring the rest of the juice to a boil. Slowly pour into dissolved flakes, stirring continuously.

→ Chill until firm.

Wild Things

{
HERBS

SEAWEEDS

SPROUTING

CULTURE

☙ HERBS

Herbs grow everywhere. Many are hanging out right now in your backyard. Herbs are more nutritious than cultivated foods: 1) They are free of pesticides; 2) their seed is natural or free of genetic modification; and 3) their soil is free from persistent nutrient-depleting farming methods.

One overlooked herb is dandelion. Dandelion has a flavor similar to mustard greens and is packed with valuable nutrients. It has a reputation for being a liver cleanser and is said to purify blood, improve skin tone, and support digestion. Cook tender young leaves as you would any other greens, but with an added step: Cook dandelion greens *twice*—steam them, drain the liquid, and then sauté them. Otherwise, they may taste bitter.

Red clover is another herbal powerhouse. Like dandelion, red clover possesses blood purifying and organ-cleansing properties. It has been used in aiding pregnancy and in rebuilding strength after illness or surgery. Red clover is also touted as an anticancer herb, made famous by Jason Winter's tea. Use any part of the plant in tea.

If you are interested in including these long-ignored yet highly praised food sources, do some research. Find out which herbs and weeds are edible, and experiment. Wild foods are like sprouts; they possess tremendous life force—vibrant and untamed—and are packed with nutrient density.

TIP: Choose herbs that thrive locally. They will offer you nutrients for *you* to thrive in *your* environment.

ર SEAWEED

Seaweeds are sea vegetables—packed with minerals, enzymes, and many nutrients. They offer some of the highest sources of vegetarian calcium and vitamin B12, both typically notorious "animal-source" nutrients. Add dry seaweed as a seasoning in soups, casseroles, and burgers. De-gas beans with seaweed. Rehydrate seaweed as a vegetable in meals.

How do I rehydrate seaweeds?

→ Place seaweed in a bowl.

→ Add cold water.

→ Let sit until seaweed has softens.

→ Save water for cooking liquid.

ર SPROUTING

When people understand what happens to a seed after it has sprouted, they may want to try sprouts. When they see how good they feel after they eat sprouts, they may try to grow them. Once they see how easy it is to grow sprouted foods, may they continue to grow them. (Oh, sprouts, hear my prayer.)

Why sprout? What's so good about it? It seems like a waste of time. Is it really worth it?

Sprouted foods are some of the most nutritious, easily digested foods found in nature. If you take the time to grow them, they are also less expensive than most vegetables.

Why are sprouts so good for you?

The answer lies in the biology of sprouting. Sprouting is the act of initiating life. Chemical and physical changes occur. Starches convert into energy that the plant utilizes to grow. Protein content increases, as well as B and C vitamins, and many important enzymes. Enzymes are substances that are *catalysts*—forming and completing chemical reactions among nutrients. Sprouts are one of most concentrated sources of enzymes. All raw and fermented foods contain enzymes, but sprouts seem to be particularly prolific, perhaps due to the fervency of germination.

What's the deal with enzymes?

Enzymes are chemicals that cause chemical reactions. We produce enzymes in our body, but ideally, we need more for optimal functioning. Traditionally, we would get these from live and/or fermented foods. These types of foods assist our body by contributing additional enzymes for many physiological processes, such as metabolism, catabolism, hormone regulation, memory making—the list is pretty long. Former diets were prevalent in fermented foods. Unfortunately, most contemporary societies have slipped away from including these miracle-workers in their diets. When we omit live, cultured, and fermented foods, our body has to be stingy with how it allocates its enzymes. It employs a "first things first" ideology to our physiology: Enzymes are assigned primarily for digestion. If we have any extra, then we can worry about "luxury items" like hormone regulation, memory making, cell regeneration, and all these other physiological processes that are not essential for surviving—only for thriving. If we don't have enough enzymes, our quality of life begins to suffer. If we are unable to replace cells, we age more quickly. If our capacity to consolidate memories decreases, we retain less information and fewer experiences (we literally remember less of our lives). Hormone imbalance also impairs memory and creates mood swings, limits creativity and problem solving, and reduces motivation by increasing depressive or lowered emotional states.

If we don't have enough enzymes, our quality of life begins to suffer. If we are unable to replace cells, we age more quickly.

Use sprouts as a metaphor for your life. As sprouting brings life into the seed, so too, it brings life into you.

How to Sprout:

→ Soak seeds in a jar overnight.

→ Drain the water.

→ Cover the jar with a sprouting lid. Turn the jar upside down to drain excess water throughout the day.

→ Rinse a few times a day.

What is the ratio of sprouts to water, for soaking?

About 2 to 1, water to sprouts. Soak a small handful of sprouts at a time.

TIP: Keeping sprouts near the kitchen sink reminds you to rinse them.

Why should the seeds stay moist and not wet?

Seeds will mold if too wet; they will stay dormant if too dry.

Why rinse throughout the day?

Rinsing stimulates growth, keeps the seeds moist, and prevents spoiling.

After the seeds begin to sprout, place the jar near the sunlight—a window sill perhaps. Baby sprouts like sunlight. The warmth and light promote green, happy, nutrient-dense sprouts.

ஜ LIVE CULTURE: TRUSTING YOUR GUT

Psychology Today ran an interesting article, asking us to consider, "Is Kimchi the New Prozac?" It discussed the theory that we have a second brain located in our digestive tract. This bundle of neurons functions independently from its home office, upstairs. The gut does not seem to be a franchise of the mind; it appears to have an agenda all its own. Most notably, it seems to receive *otherly* information in the form of intuition, sensory and visceral responses, and what might be deemed paranormal, metasensory, or beyond our conscious levels of cognition.

> *The gut does not seem to be a franchise of the mind; it appears to have an agenda all its own.*

Think of it as science versus religion: The northern brain values science, whereas the southern brain is "stuck" receiving the wacko religious stuff. Only, the tides are turning. Thanks to bridge-building pioneers like Candace Pert, Antonio Damasio, Richard Davidson (and yes, even Dan Brown), faith is making a comeback. When you get that gut feeling—for example, receive an "ick" response when meeting a person—science now validates that this information, while noncognitive, is still a knowing. This information—like facts and feelings—transfers electronically, through energy waves, and processes chemically, through particles. This type of information appears to be handled more efficiently through the "Office Down Under."

What does this have to do with cooking?

Look. We hire the chambermaid to clean all the hotel rooms, not just the penthouse suite, right? Maintaining a healthy digestive system promotes a healthy second brain.

We want to keep all the rooms clean—upstairs and downstairs. One way we keep the office down below clean is through culture. No, I don't mean "culture"—culinary acts of aesthetic presentation or incorporating local cuisines. I mean *live cultures*: friendly bacteria or probiotics who are the workhorses of the intestinal system. They are the difference between good customer service and being put on hold for 47 minutes. Probiotics do so much that it would, again, take another book to recite their deserved credit. But here are a few: stimulate digestion, increase nutritional absorption, promote regularity, decrease allergic reactions, improve immune system function, repair and rejuvenate healthy cells, identify damaged or malignant cell structures and influence destruction of said cells, balance blood sugar levels, balance hormone levels, and regulate mood through neuro-chemical balancing. Remember how we cook with intuition? This is the place where intuition resides.

Katz's Live Culture Sour Pickles

☞ Time frame: 1 to 4 weeks ☜

INGREDIENTS (FOR 1 GALLON / 4 LITERS):
3 to 4 pounds cucumbers:
    Small to medium size
    Whole, uncut, free of nicks, soft spots,
      and damage
    Cleaned
6 tablespoons sea salt
    Not iodized!
    Unrefined
4 heads fresh flowering dill
    OR 4 tablespoons fresh dill
    OR 4 tablespoons dried dill
4 heads or bulbs garlic
    Whole bulbs, not cloves!
Pinch of black pepper
Handful of fresh leaves, such as grapevine,
apple, cherry or other tree, or fruit bush
      (to propagate culture)

SPECIAL EQUIPMENT:
Ceramic crock or food-grade plastic bucket
Plate that fits inside crock or bucket
1-gallon / 4-liter jug filled with water, or
  other weight
Cloth cover

Nourish it! Sandor Katz' fantastic book, *Wild Fermentation* (2003) offers dozens of fermented and live-culture recipes from around the world. In honor of intuition and our second brain, I offer one real live recipe, below, adapted from Mr. Katz' book.

❧ ❧ ❧

Wild things . . . you make my colon sing . . . You make everything . . . groovy . . .

PROCESS:

1. Rinse cucumbers, taking care to not bruise them and making sure their blossoms are removed. Scrape off any remains at the blossom end. If you're using cucumbers that aren't fresh off the vine that day, soak them for a couple of hours in very cold water to freshen them.

2. Dissolve sea salt in ½ gallon of water to create brine solution. Stir until salt is thoroughly dissolved.

3. Clean the crock, then place at the bottom of it: dill, garlic, fresh leaves, and a pinch of black peppercorns.

4. Place cucumbers in the crock.

5. Pour brine over the cucumbers, place the (clean) plate over them, then weigh it down with a jug filled with water or a boiled rock. If the brine doesn't cover the weighted-down plate, add more brine mixed at the same ratio of just under one tablespoon of salt to each cup of water.

6. Keep the crock covered every day. Skim any mold from the surface, but don't worry if you can't get it all. If there's mold, be sure to rinse the plate and weight. Taste the pickles after a few days.

7. Check the crock every day. Skim any mold from the surface, but don't worry if you can't get it all. If there's mold, be sure to rinse the plate and weight. Taste the pickles after a few days.

8. Enjoy the pickles as they continue to ferment. Continue to check the crock every day.

9. Eventually, after one to four weeks (depending on the temperature), the pickles will be fully sour. Continue to enjoy them, moving them to the fridge to slow down fermentation.

Adapted from *Wild Fermentation*, S. Katz, 2003

Rosemary

My most important culinary lesson stabbed me in the back. Once upon a time, there lived a terrible and evil teacher at the Culinary Institute of America—Chef Bagna. This chef's reputation was notorious. Stories circulated about how he would destroy everything his students would cook and assign more homework than any other teacher— five-page, double-sided, typed essays, every night! (This was 1983, folks. We didn't have computers to type papers.) Before I even entered his kitchen, he assigned me homework.

One day, our class needed some rosemary for a veal stew, so my chef sent me to Chef Bagna's kitchen. I stood in the doorway, waiting to garner his attention. Chef Bagna was screaming at a student twice his size. The boy appeared to be disintegrating into his uniform. Seeing me frozen rudely in limbo, Chef stopped in mid-sentence and sauntered over, eyes locked.

"Yes? What?"

"Excuse me, Chef Bagna. Our kitchen needs rosemary for our *Saltimbocca*. May we borrow some, please?"

He stared at me for a while. At last he said slowly, "Rosemary."

"Yes, *CHEF*!" I replied.

"Do you hahpeen to know where rosemary oreeginates, leettle gahhrl?"

"No, Chef." I replied, a bit more softly.

"You know wheech part of rosemary plant you ask for? Betty Crocker?"

"Er . . . uh . . . noo . . . uh, chef," I mumbled into my jacket.

"You wehll, after write five-page report on rosemary. Tomorrow morning. 9:00 A.M., sharp."

"Yes, Chef. Five pages, 9:00 A.M., sharp. Thank you, Chef," I mumbled quietly, leaving without any rosemary.

"Five pages, *double*-sided, *SHOEMAKER*!" he screamed as he turned his back on me.

Needless to say, I learned a lot about rosemary that night. But now my fears were confirmed. This guy was crazy, discounted women in the kitchen, and now targeted me. I grew terrified about my rotation in his kitchen.

The day arrived. My fears didn't have a clue. This man was psychotic. He screamed for eight hours straight. He slammed pots. He pushed us. He pushed people into us. He accused us of pushing him. He kicked us out of the kitchen, when we had something cooking on the stove.

"*Get out of here!*" he would sneak up behind us and shriek out of nowhere.

"But, Chef, I have something on the stove, cooki—"

"*LEAVE MY KITCHEN, GODDAMNED SHOEMAKER DON'T COME BACK!!*"

"YES, *CHEF*!" we would clamor, bolting from the room.

Kitchen work is brutal: fast-paced environment, unbearable heat, heavy lifting, rapid-fire decision making, and verbal onslaughts.

Professional kitchens are reputed to be no place for a woman. Most traditionally trained chefs still believe this.

Chef Bagna reminded us of this constantly.

Oh, how he hated women in his kitchen: He pinched our asses, called us Shoemakers and Betty Crockers, and banished us to cleaning duty. Women washed dishes, scrubbed the ovens, and mopped the floors. If we were extremely lucky, we'd be allowed to peel carrots and wash lettuce.

But really, gender didn't matter; he hated everyone equally and assumed we were all equally incompetent. And he would prove it. He turned our ovens off while things were baking. He turned the heat way up, causing things to burn. He would turn ovens on after dinner service was over when we were cleaning the kitchen. He dumped our soup down the drain. He threw food onto the floor and demanded that we start over. He ripped up our homework, gave us zeros for the day if we went to the bathroom, and gave pop quizzes on completely unrelated material—sometimes in the middle of dinner service.

"This dude is insane," we cried. "What the hell is his *problem*??"

The answer emerged as the weeks went by. Never have I been so organized or knowledgeable as I was in Chef Bagna's kitchen—not even in Master Chef Roland Henin's. I wrote five-page (double-sided) essays on food items every night. These items were used in our service each following day. I didn't just understand the procedures for the dishes we were creating; I appreciated the culture related to them. I understood *why* we were cooking what we were cooking: the regions, climate, religion, politics, etc. In Chef Bagna's class, I didn't learn how to cook; I learned to appreciate culinary art.

It was in Chef Bagna's kitchen that my appreciation for *mise en place* ignited. All knives were sharpened perfectly and consistently. If they were not, they were tossed out into the hall. I watched everything like a hawk, acutely aware of how much time I had before service, how much food I was preparing, and how much the food cost—down to the penny. If Chef turned off one of my ovens, I corrected it immediately.

This is a common problem in a kitchen. Someone will turn off an oven thinking it was left on, without checking to see if something is cooking. If you don't check your oven periodically, you might wind up with a raw (or burnt) dish. If Chef threw me out of the kitchen, I made sure someone took over my duties at my station. I covered my station's ass, let me tell you.

And it wasn't just me. All in Chef Bagna's class transformed. If they didn't, they failed and repeated his class, until they did. He taught us to never take anything for granted, to be prepared for any calamity, and despite any setbacks, to insist that the show must go on. The meal comes out as planned and on time. No excuses.

The cool thing was that the more you "got it," the more he would leave you alone. I didn't notice this right away. It was one of those invisible things, like good health; being on top of my *mise en place* became invisible. Once I was prepared for his chaos, he stopped creating chaos. He observed and responded accordingly. The true reward of a smooth-running kitchen was in being prepared no matter what. It wasn't anything glamorous. It was the absence of drama. It was balance.

Was this man insane? Some say yes. Who am I kidding . . . *everyone* said yes. I sure did. But I also admit that he worked harder than all of us. He improved every one of his students and forced us to accept excellence. He insisted that we trust in ourselves. We rose to become the best cooks that we could be.

For a month, that is. Sigh. After that, we proceeded to our next kitchen. All of Chef Bagna's hard work collapsed like the chocolate *soufflés* he'd stab when our backs were turned.

Ain't that just the way?

Thank you, Chef Bagna. You worked harder than any Chef I have ever known. You were the Lou Gosset Jr. of the Culinary Institute of America.

I am recipe-free because of you.

HOW TO FOLLOW A RECIPE

How to
Follow a Recipe

Now that you know how to NOT follow a recipe, go ahead and follow one.

Revisit some of your favorite cookbooks. You'll see how fun it is when armed with a new perspective.

Using recipes *can* be fun. They can supply a springboard for your Mish Mash. But remember . . .

. . . use recipes for inspiration rather than commandment. Be courageous; never be afraid to substitute ingredients in a recipe. Refer back to specific chapters in this book for substitutes. And when you run out of acceptable substitutes, invent your own!

You don't need someone else's permission to experiment with cooking. Let cooking be your palette. Make mistakes and welcome the lessons. Listen to your gut and retain with your brain.

Play at your own pace. Allow yourself to eat something different every day or cook for five minutes a year—whatever makes sense to you. Give yourself permission to try and fail and try and succeed and try and fail.

And try again.

Here's to you, recipe-free warriors:

It is better to cook

A little

Throughout your life

Then to desire

Yearn and fear

And never cook at all

Listen to that voice

The one that says

You can cook

The world is your kitchen

Say grace

Dig in

Fare well.

INDEX

86, 36, 41, 53

Agar Agar, 173

A Palate for Pleasure, 32

Acesulfame, 156

accessory ingredients , 19, 36, 48, 118-20

acidosis, 104

adrenaline, 152

al dente, 96

alkaloids, 66

Amazake, 158

amino acids, 57

Anatomy of the Spirit, 3

anti-cancer, 63, 66, 174

Antonio Damasio, 177

Anything worth doing is worth over-doing., 63

arthritis, 57, 66, 77, 154,

Aspartame, 156-7

Attack of the 50-foot tall Dressing, 89

B-15 (vitamin, Pangamic Acid), 63

B-17 (vitamin, laetrile), 63

Basic Creamy Dressing, 137

Basic Herb Rule, 125

Basic Recipe Formula, 76

Basic Sweet Sauce, 264

basic yeasted bread, 268

"Better to pay the grocer than the doctor", 240

Betty Crocker, 36, 282

Bing, 37, 38, 39, 49, 151

biology (sprouting), 275

biscuits, 263

blood type, 101

Bragg's Foods, 128

Bragg's Liquid Aminos, 73

brassica, 123

break (dressing), 137

brick-by-brick, 22, 148

Bridget Jones' Diary, 22

Bring to a Boil, 99

brownie, 168

Brunoises Triumvirate, 65

burn onions, 123

Café du Parc, 24, 39, 42

caffeine, 151-158

cake, 167

cancer, 2,63, 146, 152, 156,

Candace Pert, 177

capsicum, 66

Carolyn Myss, 3

Carrie Bradshaw, 5

carry-over cooking, 43, 112,162

Century Plaza, 28

cheesecake, 18, 31, 59, 171

Chef Anthony Bourdain, 30

Chef Bagna, 180

Chef Eric Ripert, 30

Chef Pierre Latuberne, 16, 24, 39, 42, 139

Chef Raymond Hoffmeister, 28

chemistry, 103, 154,161

Chiffon pie or Mousse, 171

chlorophyll, 76

chocolate, 152, 158, 168

cigarettes, 104, 152

complete rotein, 57, 60, 63, 72-3, 158,

complex carbohydrates, 134, 140, 158

cookie, 168

cooking liquid, 37, 98, 121

cooking procedures, 20, 85

cortisol, 152

cover the pot, 111

crazybusy, 1, 14, 30, 33, 39, 62-3, 108, 110, 147, 152-4

Cream of Cauliflower soup, 1, 19, 73

Crème Anglaise, 166

crisp (fruit), 173

cross-contamination, 38

cultured (fermented) foods, 158, 175-9

Cybernetics, 15

Dan Brown, 177

Deck of Cards rule, 57

(de)-gas, 77, 115-7, 175

deglazing, 99

diabetes, 75, 152-6

dirt (vitamin B-12 source), 65

distress, 150, 157

Do What You Love and The Money Will Follow, 15

Dr. Bronner's Balanced Mineral Seasoning, 74,

duxelle, 60

Eden Foods, 72

Elizabeth Gilbert, 22

empty calorie, 6, 154-5

enzymes, 9, 34, 64-5, 73, 103, 132, 135, 154, 158, 174-6

essential amino acids, 57-8, 73

eustress, 150

excessive protein, 154

FARE WELL, 14, 34, 56,188

fight-or-flight response, 152

flan, 166

Follow Your Heart, 69

Food, Inc, 56

french cuisine, 8, 24, 65

French knife, 85

friendly bacteria, 69, 104, 132, 178

gas, 77, 115-7, 175

gasoline, 103

gelatin, 173

Gingerbread, 168

glucose, 150-6

gluten, 59, 87, 161, 165

gluten-free, 54, 73

glycogen, 150-6

granola, 173

grapeseed oil, 69

gut (feeling), 6, 23, 177,

hand-held (Immersion) blender, 70, 108, 130, 133, 137-8, 147

Henkel, 85

herbal teas, 157,

herbs, 35, 73, 75, 94, 125, 135, 138-9, 147, 152, 157, 174

High Fructose Corn Syrup, 67, 155

hippies, 57

hypothalamus, 33, 155

Is Kimchi the New Prozac?, 177

Jenson's Vegetable Seasoning, 74

jolt (caffeine), 149-151

just combined, 165

Kanten, 173

Katz's Live Culture Sour Pickles, 178

Kitchen Confidential, 30

Kumbaya, 33

Kuzu, 68, 129-30, 166, 170

lactose intolerance, 158

laetrile, 63-4, 146

Le Bernardin, 30

live cultures, 178

Lou Gosset Jr., 183

love drug, 31

macronutrients, 154

Maisie Crowther, 9

main (necessary) ingredients, 18-9, 35, 48, 94, 118-20, 141

malnutrition, 154

Maria & Ricardo's, 67

marinade, 90, 94, 133-5, 141

Marlene's Market and Deli, 1, 20

Martha Beck, 22

Martha Stewart, 21

Masaru Emoto, 32

Master Chef Roland Henin, 24-27, 37, 130, 181

Max Shulman, 150

mayonnaise, 39-41, 68-70, 7-6, 138, 140

McDonald's, 105

meetz, 50-61,

mesclan, 91

metabolism, 104, 150-3, 176

methanol, 156

micronutrients, 154

Mise en Place, 13-18, 35-6, 39, 83, 94, 182

Mish Mash, 20-1, 24, 51, 161-2, 187

Molasses cookies, 168

Muffin or Quick Bread, 167

National Pasta Association, 54

nature, 8, 103, 153

Neural Growth Hormone (NGF), 31

Nightshade (plant family), 66, 123

nonessential amino acids, 57

nut milks, 147, 158,

NutraSweet, 156-7

nutrient density, 34, 62, 71, 130, 154, 158, 168, 174

oxytocin, 31

Pacific Foods, 158

pancake, 169

Pangamic Acid (B-15), 63,

paranormal, 177

pasta, 51, 54, 69

Pasta Shoppe, 54

pasteurize, 72, 158

Paycheck Principle, 34, 108

perception, 150

perfection, 123

pH, 57

phenylalanine, 156

physics, 26, 94, 96, 101, 161

pie crust, 169

popcorn, 73, 109, 113

Psycho-cybernetics, 32,

Psychology Today, 53, 177

Pumpkin pie, 170

Quality Time, 9, 32

quercetin, 77

Quick Bread or Muffin, 167

Quick grains, 110-114

Raw Apple Cider Vinegar, 72, 146

Raw Red Grape Vinegar, 72

refined foods, 72, 104-8, 149

refined grains, 105

Rice-a-Roni, 73

RJ Reynolds, 104

rolling boil, 111

Rosemary, 180

rufie, 155

Rule # 6 (The Art of Possibility), 22

saccharin, 156

Sam, 1, 31, 80

Sandor Katz, 140, 178

sandwiches, 52-3

saturated fat, 60, 62, 70, 106

sauté, 88, 97-9

seaweed, 117, 173-5

self-cannibalism, 153

sharpening steel, 85

sharpening stone, 85

Scraps equals Soufflé, 27, 37

shoemaker, 27, 43, 180-1

Short Dough, 164-6, 169-70

Slow grains, 109-10, 114

Spike, 73, 113

sprouting, 62, 116, 174-7

squalene, 72

steam, 52, 88, 95-9

Steering by Starlight, 22

stevia, 155-6

Stew Gal, 161

stir-fry, 52, 97-9

stock, 37, 94, 98, 121-5

Stone Soup, 118-20

strawberry leaves, 66

stress, 150-7

stressor, 150

sugar party, 151

Super Healthy Yummy Caeser, 139

Sweet Sauce, 164, 166-7, 170-1

tart dough, 169

The Fry Rule, 97, 125

The Hidden Messages in Water, 32

The Secret, 15

Thud, 23-4, 42

time, 14-8, 21, 25, 27, 29, 42, 62, 94-101, 124, 132-3, 137, 147, 151, 175

unfinished business, 3

unsaturated fat (non-saturated), 72, 106

uric acid, 57, 154

utility knife, 85

Wallace and Gromit, 53

Water Test, 154

Wet into Dry, 164-5, 167-9

whole grain, 62,-4, 103-8, 130, 153

whole wheat, 68, 105, 128

Wild Fermentation, 179

About the Author

SUSIE CROWTHER

Susie Crowther is a Vermont transplant, from Chicago, Illinois. Her interest in culinary art began at the age of 3, when she began playing *Mish Mash*—an improvisational game of mixing food ingredients together and hoping for something edible. This interest grew into a career, including graduating from the CIA (Culinary Institute of America), running her own catering business—*Susie's Menu*, and later, to teaching nutrition as a college professor. Currently, she plays with the passions of health, writing, and hopefully, humor. In 2013, Susie and her husband, Mark, are planning to run away to Central America. They're wondering what to do about their dogs.

Follow Susie: http://norecipecookbook.com
Contact Susie: norecipecookbook@gmail.com

The author mish mashing, at age 3

About the Artists

JULIE FALLONE

Food is my favorite subject to work with. It never complains and is almost always patient. It doesn't mind if I squirt it with ice water or run a butane torch over it. I can poke and prod to my hearts delight, it does not complain. I have lived in Connecticut, New York City, Wisconsin, Seattle, and now Kansas City. Sometimes I miss the ocean so much that my heart breaks. I love taking pictures. I love my husband and my children, but I also love taking pictures. I would like to thank Jim, Max, and Claire for knowing to never eat the prettiest food in the refrigerator.

"Too many cameras and not enough food . . ." (Sting)

Julie DuCharme Fallone
www.juliefallone.com

MAISIE CROWTHER

Mary Barnes (Goodale) "Maisie" Crowther studied drawing, painting, and printmaking and worked in clay throughout school and college, and later attended classes with artists in Cambridge and Rockport, MA, and at Marlboro College, Marlboro, VT. She has taught art in elementary schools, Community College of Vermont and University of Vermont Extension Programs. Crowther is a member of the Vermont Watercolor Society, Saxons River Art Guild, and Brattleboro West Arts. She has exhibited in solo and group shows throughout New England. Since 1990, Crowther has been instructing and coordinating the Senior Painting Group which meets at the Brattleboro Senior Center every Wednesday morning. The watercolors printed in this volume by Susan Crowther are works created by this vibrant group.

THE BRATTLEBORO SENIOR CENTER WATER-BASED MEDIA GROUP

The watercolors in this book were painted by members of the Brattleboro Senior Center Water-based Media Group, which has been meeting regularly since 1990. It began as a class instructed by Maisie Crowther, but for the past three years, artists have shared the time and space on Wednesday mornings in the spirit of the open studio. Several of the artists are members of Saxons River Art Guild, Vermont Watercolor Society, and Brattleboro West Arts.

The Brattleboro Senior Center is a division of the Brattleboro Town Recreation and Parks Department. Members of the Senior Center Group include:

Carolyn Allbee	Michael Hanley
Barb Borek	Molly Martin
Larry Bramble	Victoria Poulos
Maisie Crowther	Arlene Rec
Barbara June Dascomb	John Spicer
John Dimick	Freda Wright

MARCIA FAGELSON

Marcia Fagelson is a retired teacher who lives in Vermont and Tennessee with her husband David, a retired physician. When she was 33, she made collages from objects collected during their travels. Forty years later, she became interested in learning how Maisie Crowther created watercolor paintings and asked her for instruction. Today, her daughter Susan, the author of this book, has given Marcia a reason and the motivation to continue drawing and painting, which she now does with water-soluble colored pencils.